On 8 November 2016, Donald Trump won the American presidential election, to the surprise of many across the globe. Now that Trump is commander-in-chief of the most powerful country on earth, Americans and non-Americans alike have been left wondering what this will mean for the world. It has been claimed that Trump's foreign policy views are impulsive, inconsistent and that they were improvised on the campaign trail. However, drawing on interviews from as far back as 1980, Charlie Laderman and Brendan Simms show that this assumption is dangerously false. They reveal that Trump has had a consistent position on international trade and America's alliances since he first considered running for president in the late 1980s. Furthermore, his foreign policy views have deep roots in American history. For the new President, almost every international problem that has confronted the United States can be explained by the mistakes of its leaders. Yet, after decades of dismissing America's leaders as fools and denouncing their diplomacy, Trump must now prove that he can do better. Over the past three decades, he has been laying out in interviews, articles, books and tweets what amounts to a foreign policy philosophy. This book reveals the world view that Trump brings to the Oval Office. It shows how that world view was formed, what might result if it is applied in policy terms and the potential consequences for the rest of the world.

Charlie Laderman is Lecturer in International History at King's College London and Harrington Faculty Fellow at the Clements Center for National Security, University of Texas, Austin. He is the author of *Saving the Armenians: Humanitarian Intervention and the Search for an Anglo-America Alliance*.

Brendan Simms is Professor of the History of European International Relations at the University of Cambridge. He is the author of *Unfinest Hour* (shortlisted for the Samuel Johnson Prize), *Three Victories and a Defeat, Europe: The Struggle for Supremacy,* and *Britain's Europe: A Thousand Years of Conflict and Cooperation*.

'This book does a great service in identifying the genesis of President Trump's world view, based on his words, and considering its likely impact on the future of American foreign policy and the Western alliance.'

John Bew, author of *Realpolitik: A History*

'As the historians Charlie Laderman and Brendan Simms show in this new book, since the 1980s Trump has developed a consistent world view. It is highly critical of the dominant US global strategy since 1945 of building and maintaining a liberal capitalist international order.'

Alex Callinicos, Socialist Worker

'In this insightful study, Laderman and Simms expose the contours of Donald Trump's thinking on foreign policy and explore its roots in US history since 1945. This book refutes the widespread view that Trump can simply be dismissed as an improviser and a showman. Essential reading for anyone who wants to understand the Trump presidency and what it means for the rest of us.'

Sir Christopher Clark, author of *Sleepwalkers: How Europe Went to War in 1914*

'The unthinkable has happened: Donald Trump is now President of the United States. We can condemn, dismiss, and ridicule him. But it makes more sense to understand him. This short book uses his lifeworld and his own language to do so, and offers an insightful and compelling account of his world view, and especially his view of foreign affairs. For anybody who wants to know what makes Trump tick and how he is likely to behave this is an absolute must read.'

Richard Ned Lebow, James O. Freedman Presidential Professor Emeritus of Government, Dartmouth College

'Highly recommend this study of the development of Trump's foreign policy world view ... Instant and powerful illumination!'

Adam Tooze, author of *The Deluge: The Great War and the Remaking of Global Order 1916–1931*

'The most comprehensive account yet of Trump's thinking over the years.'

Paul D. Miller, *The American Interest*

**CHARLIE LADERMAN
AND BRENDAN SIMMS**

DONALD TRUMP

THE MAKING OF A WORLD VIEW

I.B. TAURIS

LONDON · NEW YORK

Revised edition published in 2017 by
I.B.Tauris & Co. Ltd
London • New York
www.ibtauris.com

First published by Endeavour Press Ltd, 2017

ISBN: 978 1 78831 048 2

A full CIP record for this book is available from the British Library
A full CIP record is available from the Library of Congress

Library of Congress Catalog Card Number: available

Printed and bound by CPI Group (UK) Ltd, Croydon, CR0 4YY

The convictions that leaders have formed before reaching high office are the intellectual capital they will consume as long as they continue in office.

Henry Kissinger, US Secretary of State, 1979

CONTENTS

PREFACE

The world hungers for information on, and understanding of, Donald Trump, especially his foreign policy vision. Around the globe, people awaited his inauguration – some anxiously, others eagerly, but few indifferently. Existing biographies of Trump are not only mostly partisan, in both directions, but they all focus almost exclusively on his remarkable business career and colourful personal life. There has been some excellent recent commentary on Trump's foreign policy, particularly as the growing possibility and ultimate reality of him becoming president began to dawn; however, much of the analysis of Trump's world view is based primarily on his campaign statements. There is no monograph that explores the coherence of Trump's views over time or examines them in their proper historical context.

We hope that the information contained in this book will enable readers to make up their own minds about the new President's foreign policy. For that purpose, we have attempted to present that view, as much as possible, in Trump's own words, relying primarily on interviews that

Trump has given over more than three decades. For most incoming presidents, commentators and scholars have an extensive oeuvre to draw on; from voting records and policies enacted or supported, to articles in foreign policy publications or detailed treatises on international affairs. As Donald Trump was the first person to assume the presidency with no prior political or military experience, those seeking to understand his world view must look elsewhere. Consequently, we have mined Trump's statements and remarks on foreign affairs over the past three-and-a-half decades in an attempt to understand whether there are any convictions, formed over time, that will undergird his diplomatic policies and strategic outlook in office. As historians, we have attempted to contextualise these comments, offering insights into the broader political background to the statements and, as far as possible, have examined them in relation to Trump's own personal and business situation at the time. As historians, we have also sought to explore Trump's world view and previous foreign policy recommendations with reference to the broader sweep of American foreign policy since World War II and offer observations as to how his world view compares and contrasts with that of his predecessors. And as historians, we are also well aware that US presidents do not always develop in ways expected of them on the basis of their previous statements, something which has been particularly true for foreign policy. Yet we also know from our study of history that there is little time for leaders to learn on the job. As Henry Kissinger has stated, it is the core convictions that presidents formed prior to entering government that "they will consume as long as they continue in office." This book is an attempt to ascertain what convictions Donald Trump, the 45th President of the United States, will bring to the White House.

The book begins with two brief analytical chapters. The second half consists of verbatim extracts and paraphrased sections of Trump's public statements on international affairs, prefaced by commentary. We also provide links to the full text for readers who wish to read or hear the extracts in their original context. Unlike some of the recent compendia of Trump's statements during the campaign, our principal concern here is not to judge their "truth content." Instead, we will pay particular attention to speeches and especially the numerous long interviews, which reveal the "pure" Trump, rather than his books, which have been largely ghost-written. We focus on the period from his first recorded foreign policy statement in 1980 to 2014, because we thereby get a much better sense of his "bedrock" beliefs, shorn of tactical considerations for the 2016 presidential election. The final chapters will show the remarkable consistency of Trump's thought over time and suggest what it might mean for the world order over the next four to eight years. We shall repeat ourselves, because he has done so over three decades. That is something worth repeating, again and again, until everyone has taken it on board.

ACKNOWLEDGEMENTS

The authors wish to thank those who helped to put this book together for a tight deadline: Constance Simms, Anita Bunyan, Rhonda Laderman, Daniel Laderman, Patrick Laderman, William Inboden, Tom Wright, Tom Grant, Ionut Popescu, Paul Miller, Jacqueline Chandler, Ian Johnson, Chris Miller, Catherine Evans, Jennifer Johnson, Jeremi Suri, Mark Lawrence, Andrew Preston, John Thompson, John Bew and various other figures who wish to remain anonymous, all of whom have offered counsel and assistance. Steven McGregor and Ashlyn Webb have been wonderful research assistants, sourcing documents and providing excellent insights. The support, guidance and advice of Emily Charnock has been absolutely invaluable to the project. We would also like to thank Jason Cowley of the *New Statesman*, Paul Lay at *History Today*, Cameron Abadi at *Foreign Policy* and Orlando Radice at *The Jewish Chronicle* for the opportunity to road-test some of these ideas. It goes without saying that all errors are the sole responsibility of the authors.

INTRODUCTION
PLAYING THE FOOL

When Donald Trump was born on 14 June 1946, the power of the United States was unprecedented. It had come out of World War II as the wealthiest and strongest nation in the world. It was the only major nation to emerge from the war vastly richer rather than much poorer and its standard of living was higher than that in any other country. Its per capita Gross Domestic Product (GDP) exceeded that of any other nation. Its manufacturing production accounted for over half of the global total and it was responsible for a third of the world's production of goods. On top of this, the United States possessed an exceptional military arsenal. Its navy was unrivalled, its air power was unsurpassed and, at the time, it alone possessed the atomic bomb – a weapon whose awesome power had just devastated Hiroshima and Nagasaki. The world had never before seen economic and strategic power on this scale.[1]

In Trump's formative years, however, Americans were forced to come to terms with the fact that America's power, though considerable, had its limits. Many Americans look back on the 1950s as a golden time in US history, an era when the nation was secure, self-confident and supreme in its global hegemony. Yet as Harry Truman prepared to leave the White House in 1952, the United States was mired in the Korean War and Americans were angry at their government, alarmed by their nation's military performance and anxious about the country's position in the world. Despite possessing unparalleled power and prosperity, the United States was struggling to secure victory on the Korean peninsula and the Truman administration was being accused of having "lost" China, after Mao Zedong established a Communist regime in 1949. Writing in the lead up to the 1952 presidential election, the British historian D.W. Brogan summed up the prevailing American attitude. Across the United States, Brogan observed widespread disbelief that there were areas of the world where America's power did not extend. Instead, Americans blamed its setbacks on the incompetence of their elected and non-elected officials. As Brogan noted, many Americans held to "the illusion that any situation which distresses or endangers the United States only exists because some Americans have been fools or knaves."[2]

Donald Trump was a child of the 1950s and, just as his domestic agenda is a nod to that era's vision of the American Dream, his world view reflects the mentality that Brogan identified. For Trump, almost every international problem that beset the United States was explained by the idiocy of its leaders. For decades, he claimed that America's politicians were being duped by the rest of the world. In his 1987 open letter to the American people, when Trump bullishly inserted himself into national politics for the first time, Trump declared that "the world is laughing at America's politicians."[3] The same day that letter appeared, he told Larry King in a CNN interview that other countries "laugh at us behind our backs, they laugh at us because of our stupidity and [that of our] leaders."[4] He has been repeating that refrain ever since.

Convinced that the United States is losing out in international trade, Trump declares: "Free trade can be wonderful if you have smart people, but we have people that are stupid. We have people that aren't smart."[5] In its alliances, Trump says, the US is "defending wealthy nations for nothing, nations that would be wiped off the face of the earth in about fifteen minutes if it weren't for us," while they "laugh at our stupidity."[6] On America's immigration policy, Mexico is "laughing at us, at our stupidity."[7] On the environment, while "China and other countries, they just burn whatever the hell is available," the United States adhered to international regulations because "our leaders are stupid, they are stupid people."[8] When oil prices rose in the 1980s and 1990s, Trump suggested that "the cartel kept the price up, because, again, they were smarter than our leaders."[9] And the fact that the United States did not "reimburse" itself and its allies by taking Iraq's oil before its withdrawal in 2011 is because "our politicians are so stupid that they've never even thought of it."[10] For decades, under Republican and Democratic administrations, Trump blamed virtually every international development that negatively impacted the United States on the foolishness of America's leaders.

According to Trump, this idiocy has turned the United States into a perpetual loser in international affairs. Just like the Americans who were frustrated in the 1950s that no clear triumph had occurred in Korea, Trump has consistently complained that "we don't win anymore." One example among many was Trump's declaration when announcing his campaign for presidency in 2015 that "we don't have victories anymore. We used to have victories, but [now] we don't have them."[11] Trump's message resonated with voters because, ever since the Korean War, many Americans have shared his bewilderment and outrage that America's overwhelming military and economic power has not translated into decisive victories. The clearest example was the war in Vietnam where despite half-a-million American ground troops, technological superiority and success in conventional battles, the United States was forced into an ignominious withdrawal. Even when the United States has crushed an adversary, such as in the first Gulf War, a decisive victory has proved elusive. Indeed, large numbers of US troops have been stationed in the Middle East ever since. And since 11 September 2001 the United States has been engaged in a "War on Terror" that has involved seemingly interminable military engagement overseas. For Trump, who told Rona Barrett in a 1980 interview that he looks at life as "combat," endless struggle with no clear victory is intolerable.[12]

In Trump's view, for the United States to become a "winner" again and reassert its "greatness," all that is required is effective leadership. As he remarked to Barrett over 30 years ago, "I feel that this country with the proper leadership can go on to become what it once was, and I hope, and certainly hope, that it does go on to be what it should be."[13] In 1987, Trump took out a full page advertisement in three major newspapers to present these views. As the headline accompanying it proclaimed: "There's nothing wrong with America's Foreign Defense Policy that a little backbone can't cure."[14]

Trump is a believer in the power of human agency to bring about fundamental change, particularly when that agent is Trump himself. As he put it in a 1990 interview with *Playboy*: "People need ego, whole nations need ego. I think our country needs more ego, because it is being ripped off so badly by our so-called allies."[15] And, after many years of flirting with the presidency, in 2015 Trump declared that "our country needs a truly great leader, and we need a truly great leader now. We need a leader that wrote *The Art of the Deal*.[16] He had clearly decided, as he put it at the 2016 Republican Convention when accepting the party's nomination for president, "I alone can fix it."[17] After decades of lambasting America's leaders as fools, Trump now has to prove that he can do a better job.

Yet for his opponents, it is Trump who is the real fool. They have repeatedly ridiculed him as a joke, a clown, a modern day P.T. Barnum, who is shameless in the stunts that he is willing to pull to keep himself in the public eye. Trump certainly portrays himself as a showman. But, as a result, his critics have failed to engage seriously with his world view. As the journalist Salena Zito succinctly put it during the 2016 campaign, while Trump's supporters "take him seriously, but not literally … the press takes him literally, but not seriously."[18] In this book, we intend to take Trump seriously and, while not always literally, where possible we will allow his words to speak for themselves.

Over the past three decades, Trump has been laying out in interviews, articles, books and tweets what amounts to a foreign policy philosophy. For most of that period, he has been roundly mocked by pundits and politicians, and his positions widely dismissed. If Trump's views could be ignored in the past, it is a long time since that was possible. Unless his opponents seriously engage with Trump's world view, he will continue to play them for fools.

CHAPTER 1

IMPERIAL OVERSTRETCH: THE INTELLECTUAL ROOTS OF TRUMPISM ABROAD

During the 2016 US presidential campaign, the conventional wisdom about Donald Trump ran something like this: Trump is a buffoon. His solutions to world problems are not policies at all, but just a set of contrarian reflexes. He is, they said, a mere pied piper whose "deplorable" followers suffer from false consciousness about their true economic interest. Trump's election would be a disaster, the argument ran, but his policies will soon prove impracticable.

This conventional view, we believe, was and still is wrong. Though Trump's personal behaviour is often clownish or boorish, and he has shown astonishing ignorance of some major world issues, he has articulated a set of basic stances on foreign policy. And he has clung to them with remarkable consistency over many years in the public spotlight and now in the White House. He stands for the protection of American jobs at home and therefore for a restrictive trade policy abroad. He wants to get tough on terrorism, and is willing to countenance torture, in both the United States and the rest of the world. He wants to increase military spending, while making other countries pay more for American protection. Above all, he wants to "put America First," eschewing "nation building" abroad and de-emphasising the US role in maintaining the liberal, global order in favour of investment in security and infrastructure at home.

We should not assume that this is just rhetoric. First, because – as we shall show – Trump has been saying all this, or much of it, for more than 30 years in his writings and interviews. He is no mere opportunist. Secondly, because Trump's foreign policy positions have a long history in American politics. His stump speeches were a concoction of nationalist, nativist, protectionist, populist, isolationist and militarist elements. As the scholar Walter Russell Mead has noted, in the American foreign policy tradition, Trump's stance and, more fundamentally, the attitude of his supporters, most closely corresponds with that of Andrew Jackson, the seventh president of the United States. "Jacksonians," as Mead defines them, are focused on safeguarding the physical security and economic welfare of the American nation against those it regards as its enemies at home and abroad. They have a populist suspicion of the elite establishment, who they regard as insufficiently patriotic and more concerned with abstract cosmopolitan ideals than prioritising the citizens of their own nation. They have little interest in ensuring the spread of democratic or capitalist values around the world and, in general, are little concerned with foreign affairs unless the nation is attacked and then they respond with overwhelming force, evincing little regard for legal conventions and utter revulsion for those who wish to respond proportionately or in a limited fashion to perceived threats. Jackson's legacy has had a significant impact on US foreign policy, particularly during the nineteenth century. However, while the Jacksonian perspective has continued to have a considerable impact on public attitudes to foreign affairs, especially during times of conflict, it had relatively little influence on how policymakers conceived of US grand strategy in the 70 years after World War II, as successive administrations saw America's international role as the leader of a liberal, global order. Yet, with Trump's election victory, at the head of what Mead has called a "Jacksonian Revolt," this tradition is now resurgent.[1]

When contemplating Trump, critics have tended to focus on his domestic consequences. They see the elevation of white supremacist discourses to a kind of respectability or "normalisation," and point to an uptick in hate crimes, especially against Muslims. But in the longer term, the threat Trump poses to politics within the United States is probably overstated. His campaign and presidency thus far has undoubtedly contributed to an increase in racial tension, but American society is resilient, diverse and, for the most part, fundamentally decent. The United States is not seriously at risk of lapsing into the kind of populist authoritarianism we see in other parts of the world. Moreover, the nature of the US Constitution is such that Trump is, at least partially, constrained in what he can do at home; by Congress, by the courts and various other checks and balances. There are far fewer impediments, however, to presidential power in foreign policy. Since so much of Trump's domestic programme depends on what he does abroad, this means that the rest of the world is much more exposed to a Trump Presidency than Americans themselves.

The essence of Trump's vision for the world is the revival of American national greatness. He wants to "make America great again." "Americanism" he says, "not globalism will be our credo."[2] There was much talk during the campaign of the domestic nativism that has traditionally underpinned this slogan, "America First". But the other side of the "America First" rallying cry in US history is its opposition to international political commitments, suspicion of foreign alliances and appeal for a more narrowly nationalistic atttiude to foreign policy. The language of "America First" was first employed in presidential campaigns in the twentieth century by the Democrat Woodrow Wilson's supporters in 1916 to emphasise that he had kept the US out of World War I.[3] Wilson's use of the term was a broader one, however, and aimed to ensure

American neutrality in the conflict so that it could help aid the cause of post-war peace. The phrase took on its more nationalist, inward-looking form when it was taken up by his Republican successor Warren Harding in 1920 to channel American disillusionment with its ultimate involvement in the war in Europe and in defiance of Wilson's call for the US to join the League of Nations. Harding told Americans that he was "thinking of America first … safety, as well as charity, begins at home."[4] The most notorious use of the term was by the "America First Committee," which formed in September 1940 in opposition to President Franklin Roosevelt's commitment to aid Britain and its allies against Nazi Germany. The organisation attracted controversy due to the bigotry and anti-Semitism espoused by some of its members and there was an outcry after its leading spokesperson, Charles Lindbergh, claimed American Jews were pushing the US into war with Hitler. But its central message, that the US should refrain from external commitments and build a "Fortress America" that would make the country invulnerable to external threats, enjoyed considerable public support.[5]

After the Japanese assault on Pearl Harbor brought the US into World War II, the "America First" banner was associated with a discredited ideology and did not reappear in a national campaign until Patrick Buchanan revived it during his run for the 1992 Republican presidential nomination. In the first presidential election since the fall of the Berlin Wall, Buchanan called for a complete withdrawal of US forces from Europe and condemned President George H.W. Bush for involving the US in the first Gulf War, which he claimed was incited by Israel and its "amen corner" in the US.[6] Trump, in fact, explicitly distanced himself, in the lead up to the 2000 presidential campaign, when he was considering running for the Reform Party, from his rival Buchanan's suggestion that Hitler had not directly threatened the United States before Roosevelt took the country into World War II.[7] But by unabashedly adopting the "America First" slogan in 2016, Trump nevertheless appealed to a foreign policy tradition with deep roots in American history. In short, by contrast with every single Democratic and Republican President since World War II, including George W. Bush, Trump rejects the international liberal order.

At the heart of Trump's revolt against that order, undoubtedly, is economics. Reviving the American economy is essential to making America great again. Central to that project is a revision of the terms of trade. Trump is convinced that the US is getting a raw deal, not just from its enemies, but also – and most importantly – from its friends.

Trump's grand strategy might begin with economics and trade but it does not end there. Trump has repeatedly questioned whether Washington should continue to protect its allies in Europe and Asia, unless they contribute more to compensate the US for the expense. His ire has been directed, in particular, at America's NATO allies, most of whom fail to pay their agreed contribution to the common defence. Here – unlike with South Korea and Japan, who largely pay their way on defence, contributing large sums to support the stationing of US troops on their soil – President Trump would have a valid point if he was simply urging America's European allies to uphold their commitment to spend at least 2 per cent of GDP on defence. What Trump's pre-presidential rhetoric actually seemed to suggest, however, is that America's allies should pay a kind of "tribute" to it for the stationing of US forces in their region. Back in 1987, Trump declared that America's "world protection is worth hundreds of billions of dollars to these countries" and that the US could "end our huge deficits" if it forced its allies to "pay for the protection we extend."[8] He has regularly rehashed that argument over the intervening decades. Rather than a mutually beneficial alliance, Trump's conception of NATO appears to be more nakedly transactional, whereby the US extracts financial compensation from its associates in exchange for protection.

There is a certain irony here. For many years, leftist critics of US foreign policy have claimed (largely incorrectly as the historian John Thompson has demonstrated) that the desire to establish and underwrite a liberal international economic order stemmed inevitably from its capitalist political economy.[9] Now here is Donald Trump, America's most high profile capitalist, stating his intention to dismantle that order because it is not profitable for the US and disowning foreign interventions because they have not materially benefited the US. In fact, Trump's critique that the multilateral trading system and liberal political order established by the United States in the 1940s has not been geared *exclusively* towards advancing America's own economic prosperity is not wrong. As Thompson has shown, the US actively promoted agreements that discriminated against American exports, such as the European Payments Union, and during the Cold War it continued to station US troops overseas even when this caused balance of payments problems.[10] But that is because US foreign policy since World War II has, on the whole, not been primarily motivated by the desire to advance American economic interests, narrowly defined.

In fact, the US has regularly sacrificed jobs at home and trade advantages abroad to promote prosperity in the rest of the free world. Nor has US foreign policy been driven by a limited conception of national security. Rather, what has undergirded America's global role is the belief that the nation's unprecedented power brought with it the responsibility and opportunity to fashion an international order that advanced a broader conception of America's national interest, security and prosperity. That order, based on the rule of law and economic openness, was designed to ensure that international trade flourishes and that the United States was not embroiled in a large-scale regional inter-state conflict, such as occurred in World War I and World War II. International political stability depends on US leadership; it is underpinned by US alliances with over 60 countries across the globe and American military bases in 65 states, helping to deter would-be aggressors and enabling US forces to be forwardly present to act against potential threats.[11] It is an order that certainly benefits the United States, if not always strictly materially. But it benefits America's allies immeasurably more. And that is why the implementation of Trump's world view, if it leads to the United States retreating from its international commitments, is potentially so damaging to the health of the global order and, ultimately, to the survival of the free world.

It would be wrong to hope that either domestic or international checks and balances will constrain Trump abroad. The executive is bound to obey most of his orders in theory and probably all of them in practice. It is true that the US military, the Central Intelligence Agency (CIA) and law enforcement officers might, as former Director of the CIA, Mike Hayden suggested, refuse to follow an "illegal" order. It is also possible that Congress might hold up international trade measures in so far as they relate to treaties. Broad congressional opposition to Trump's proposed plans to downgrade support for Ukraine might provide the basis for Congress to counter any plans that the new president has for a Détente 2.0 with Russia, just as it was able to stymie the original détente in the 1970s.

This is wishful thinking. Key questions, such as whether to deliver on a NATO Article 5 security guarantee in Europe are, for good reasons, matters to be decided by the executive alone. Congress can prevent Trump from repealing an existing treaty, and can attach provisions to new ones, but it could not, for example, make him defend the Baltic members of NATO against a Russian attack. In addition, Congress has not officially declared war since the US entrance into World War II and since then the executive has enjoyed considerable freedom in deciding where and when to deploy US forces around the world.

In short, Trump has already delivered a severe shock to both the United States and the world. At home however, there are clear limits to what he can achieve. Abroad, there are far fewer constraints. What follows is an attempt to understand where Donald Trump's world view came from, unpack its core themes and evaluate its implications for the rest of the world.

CHAPTER 2

NOVICE: WEALTH AND THE NATION, 1980–2000

Nobody embodied the culture of 1980s American materialism and Wall Street capitalism like Donald Trump. As the British journalist Polly Toynbee put it after interviewing him in 1988, "Donald Trump is New York. Glitz, greed, glamour and an ambition so colossal that it will probably not rest until he rules the world – which one day he just might."[1] Trump's status as the personification of the nation's get-rich-quick ethos was cemented at the beginning of the decade when he gave his first major television interview to Rona Barrett on NBC. The interview was part of a special series on the "self-made rich in America." Leaving aside the fact that Trump had received a substantial loan from his real estate developer father to start his business, his ambitious forays into real estate ventures in Manhattan had caused a considerable stir in New York and, he boasted to

Barrett, made him "a billionaire at 34."[2] Yet Trump's interview with Barrett ranged well beyond real estate. For the first time, Trump would also provide a national audience with an insight into his world view. The themes raised in this interview would resound in Trump's foreign policy rhetoric for the rest of the decade and beyond.

The context in which Trump's 1980 interview with Barrett took place is important. It occurred the month before the 1980 presidential election. For the past four years, President Jimmy Carter had struggled to address an economic crisis that had begun under Richard Nixon. Inflation and unemployment had skyrocketed. On the international stage, the United States was on the back-foot in the Cold War as the Soviet Union spread its influence into the Horn of Africa, Central America and the Middle East. By 1979, Carter's popularity had plummeted as he came to symbolise, for many Americans, a sense of national malaise, defeatism and a declining confidence in America's destiny. The nadir came in November 1979 when, months after America's ally the Shah of Iran had been overthrown in a revolution, the US embassy in Tehran was assaulted and its diplomats and Marine guards taken hostage. While the television networks daily reminded Americans how long the crisis had lasted, Carter refrained from conducting normal business until the hostages were released, only serving to magnify the influence of the kidnappers. After initially indicating his willingness to negotiate with the Iranians, Carter ultimately bowed to public pressure and authorised a military rescue attempt, but it was badly bungled. In total, the hostage crisis stretched out over 444 days and was still going on when Trump sat down for his interview with Barrett.

Like so many Americans of his generation, Trump's world view was shaped by the trauma of the hostage crisis and the sense of US decline in the late 1970s and 1980s. He also shared the widespread sense that America's allies were not pulling their weight, in Europe, Asia and the Middle East, and that these "friends" were taking unfair advantage of the United States with respect to trade. In September 1987, Trump paid almost $95,000 to take out a full-page newspaper advertisement that ran in the *New York Times* and several other outlets to air his grievances with America's leaders and its allies. The advert was an open letter to the American people that criticised successive US governments for "paying to defend countries that can afford to defend themselves."[3] Already famous in the US and around the world as a multi-millionaire real estate developer, this letter was the opening gambit in Trump's first flirtation with running for high office.

Coming at a time of widespread concern about the huge rises in the US federal budget deficit and before Americans realised that their principal geopolitical competitor, the Soviet Union, was on the verge of collapse, Trump's letter reflected a widespread anxiety in American society. Many Americans feared that their country was in terminal decline and would soon be overtaken by a rival. Japan, whose economy was surging at this time, was the nation that many pundits predicted could take the place of the United States as the number one power in world affairs.[4] The book that captured the spirit of the moment was Paul Kennedy's landmark study, *The Rise and Fall of the Great Powers* (1987). Drawing on 500 years of international history, Kennedy's book expertly explored the relationship between economic power and military might. It concluded with a warning that the US was at risk of "imperial overstretch" because the "sum total of the United States' global interests and obligations is nowadays far larger than the country's power to defend them all simultaneously."[5] Kennedy's scholarly study offered a historically informed insight into the American predicament and proved to be a publishing sensation. It soared as high as second place on the *New York Times* non-fiction bestseller list. The book at number one? Donald Trump's memoir, *Trump: The Art of the Deal*.

Kennedy's book was also a bestseller in Japan, where it was seen as predicting Japan's imminent ascendancy to number one status. Japan's economic transformation since its crushing defeat in World War II and occupation by the United States had been stark. It had grown on average at 10.5 per cent a year between 1950 and 1973, aided in no small part by the fact that it spent relatively little on its defence; the legal basis for this was its American drafted, post-war constitution that determined that it would be a "demilitarised" country and the 1951 US–Japan security treaty, which sanctioned America's military presence on its territory. Benefitting from America's strategic protection, the US Navy's commitment to keeping open its sea lanes and an international trading order that depended on the leadership of the United States, Japan's leaders could concentrate on building an economy that grew at a startling rate and was the envy of the rest of the world. There were, of course, many other reasons besides the fact that Japan sheltered under the American strategic umbrella to explain its economic success and experts have emphasised various cultural, sociological, technical, political, educational and fiscal reasons.[6] Nevertheless, there was a widespread American perception, which Trump expressed particularly vociferously, that the US, despite its own economic travails, was defending a wealthy competitor and being taken advantage of by its "so-called ally."[7]

Boosted by its determination to keep its currency at an artificially low level, Japan's exports flooded into markets across the world as it became the dominant producer in a bewildering array of industries, particularly new high technology products. Its automobile industry was responsible for almost a quarter of the world's global production by the mid 1980s. However, many foreign manufacturers were prevented by various formal and informal constraints from gaining access to Japanese markets. The glaring exception were the raw materials on which Japan depended, notably its reliance on foreign sources for 99 per cent of its oil. In a remarkably short period, Japan also emerged as the world's leading creditor nation, as its banks expanded their influence across the world. At the same time, the United States just as rapidly had been transformed from the largest lender nation to the biggest borrower.[8]

With Japan's booming wealth came calls for restrictions on the flow of their goods into American markets and Trump was vocal in that campaign, as the documents in this chapter suggest. He also railed against the low amounts that Japan spent on defence and castigated American leaders for allowing them to "free ride" and rely on US protection. In fact, Japan had been making payments since 1978 to defray the cost of maintaining US bases on their territory, ultimately amounting to around a third of the expense for supporting the almost 50,000 troops stationed there.[9] At the same time, the US government was pressuring Japan to help share the burden of defending East Asia and raise its defence spending to around 3–4 per cent of GDP – the same amount that it was endeavouring to get its European NATO allies to spend.[10] However, any attempt to get the Japanese to spend more on defence came up against the constitutional constraints that precluded sending troops abroad and the nation's entrenched anti-militarism since World War II. Memories of the horrors of the 1930s and 1940s ensured that there was little appetite amongst Japan's neighbours for expanding its military presence in the region. Of course, there was also opposition from Japanese elites to raising the deficit or increasing taxes to pay for defence spending. In any case, these Japanese objections were received with disdain by many disgruntled Americans who disliked the fact that the burden for defending the region and protecting the Pacific sea lanes fell overwhelmingly on the United States. It was this context that provided the backdrop to Trump's first major policy intercession and it was a theme that would continue to animate his rhetoric over the coming years, even as he shifted his focus from Japan to other nations.

One of the great surprises is the relative lack of interest in the East–West conflict in the 1980s, even though anxieties about the waning of American power in the face of Moscow's global activism were very much part of the context in which Trump's pronouncements were received. Trump himself made only glancing reference to Russia, and while no apologist for communism, rated other threats to the United States more highly. He seems, in fact, to have seen himself as a peace-maker on the subject of nuclear weapons at least, perhaps a portent of his current hope to bring Washington and Moscow together.

Trump does not seem to have joined in the triumphalism of the 1990s, the American "unipolar moment" after victory in the Cold War. This may be partly explained in the early years of the decade by his focus on addressing his financial difficulties and dealing with the fallout from his high-profile divorce. Indeed, in this period it was Trump, rather than the United States, that experienced the consequences of "imperial overstretch." However, even after his high profile "comeback," Trump seemed less willing to intervene in foreign policy discussions than previously. Yet when he did return to the national political scene in the lead up to the 2000 election, when he entertained the idea of running for president on the Reform party ticket, we see the same sense of decline and lost respect in his rhetoric. This despite the fact that many would regard the year 2000 as the apotheosis of US global power. One way or another, most of the foreign policy themes associated with Donald Trump during the 2016 campaign were visible three decades earlier, with the exception of immigration and, perhaps, terrorism.

Overall, two other things stand out. First, Trump has a strong sense of life as "struggle," which he transfers from the business to the political sphere. Secondly, Trump's presidential ambitions have been visible from the start and they have always been closely connected to his view of America's place in the world. It is surely no coincidence that most of his interventions since 1980 have coincided with the electoral cycle. That said, Trump seems at first to have to have seen himself as a John the Baptist, crying in the wilderness, but not necessarily the messiah that would lead the United States into the promised land.

Interview with Rona Barrett, NBC, "Rona Barrett Looks at Today's Super Rich," 6 October 1980.[11]

This is Donald Trump's earliest recorded statement on foreign policy to a national audience, made in the dying days of the Carter administration. He states that his personal philosophy rests on seeing "life to a certain extent as combat," reflecting his Hobbesian perspective on international affairs, in which the world is anarchic and strength is paramount. Some central foreign policy preoccupations are already visible. The emphasis on "respect" as the basis of his foreign policy outlook was to endure for the rest of his career. As Polly Toynbee would point out in a 1988 interview, this obsession with "respect" leaves Trump sounding like a character out of *The Godfather*, a film that Trump has said is a favourite.[12] According to Trump, "respect" for the United States and a more active American role in the Middle East would have prevented Iran from capturing and holding American hostages. Although Trump does not specify how, he also states that a stronger American posture would have precluded the Iran–Iraq War, which had broken out a couple of weeks before this interview and would last for most of the 1980s, turning into the largest conventional war of the twentieth century and causing over 1 million casualties. What is clear from this interview is the stress that Trump places on America's power, if it is underpinned by effective leadership and national will, to shape the world as it wishes.

The war in Vietnam shapes the context in which Trump's interview with Barrett took place, as it did almost all discussions of foreign affairs for a generation of Americans. Trump did not serve in Vietnam, receiving four deferments on educational grounds and one for heel spurs.[13] He was unable, however, to escape the pervasive impact that America's inability to defeat the Vietcong had on discussions on subsequent US overseas interventions. After Barrett compared his Iran hostage plan with the use of American helicopters to rescue civilians after the Fall of Saigon in 1975, Trump states that he sees fewer challenges in the Iranian case, dismissing their army as "non-existent" and expressing confidence that American military power could overcome any obstacles. Surprisingly, even though the Soviet Union appeared to be on the advance across the world during this period, Trump makes no mention of Moscow or the broader Cold War context.

The interview does reveal, for the first time, Trump's fixation with Middle Eastern oil. The Iranian Revolution and the Iran–Iraq War had led to a surge in the price of oil in 1979–80, the second great hike after that caused by the 1973–4 embargo imposed by the Organization of Petroleum Exporting Countries (OPEC) following the Yom Kippur War. While the US had been the principal producer of world oil at the time of Trump's birth, by the 1970s it had been overtaken by the Middle Eastern nations, particularly Saudi Arabia, and fears were growing that existing US reserves would soon run out. The US began importing more of its oil, and while it was far less reliant on Middle Eastern supplies than Japan or the Western European nations, it was still susceptible to price rises by OPEC, which was increasingly controlled by the Middle Eastern nations.[14] Trump's vision that an American intervention would make it an "oil-rich nation" would re-emerge in other contexts over the coming years.

Despite Trump's impassioned critique of American foreign policy, he makes clear to Barrett that he is not yet interested in running for the presidency as he regards politics as a "mean life." Strikingly, for someone who was often labelled a populist in the 2016 presidential campaign, Trump claims that his opposition to entering public life partly stems from his belief that his views "may be right but may be unpopular." Moreover, for someone who would go on to become the first reality TV star to become president, he also agrees with Barrett that television has "hurt the political process" and laments that Abraham Lincoln would not be currently "electable because of television." Nevertheless, what is first apparent here is Trump's abiding belief that "there is one man that can turn this country around" and that the nation's real "leaders" are in the business world rather than politics.

BARRETT: *Is respect the most important thing in your opinion?*

TRUMP: *Respect can lead to other things. When you get the respect of the other countries, then the other countries tend to do a little bit as you do, and you can create the right attitudes. The Iranian situation is a case in point. That they hold our hostages is just absolutely, and totally ridiculous. That this country sits back and allows a country such as Iran to hold our hostages, to my way of thinking, is a horror, and I don't think they'd do it with other countries. I honestly don't think they'd do it with other countries.*

BARRETT: *Obviously you're advocating that we should have gone in there with troops, et cetera, and brought our boys out like Vietnam.*

TRUMP: *I absolutely feel that, yes. I don't think there's any question, and there is no question in my mind. I think right now we'd be an oil-rich nation, and I believe that we should have done it, and I'm very disappointed that we didn't do it, and I don't think anybody would have held us in abeyance …*

BARRETT: *There is a war raging there right now.*

TRUMP: *Oh yes, there is a war, and it's a war where nobody has any tanks, has any guns. It's a war where everyone is standing around. That would have been the easiest victory we would have ever won, in my opinion.*

BARRETT: *Well, when I look at television, I see men being shot up like being blown off.*

TRUMP: *But you're talking about two non-existent armies. I mean Iran has an army composed of American equipment without parts and without anything else, and Iraq has a very weak army, and they're just really fighting each other, and it's almost hand-to-hand combat if you see now. It's a sad situation, Rona, but it's a situation which ultimately is going to get much worse. That little sparkle of war, that little sparkle, is going to lead in my opinion to a much, much greater conflict, and I think that's very unfortunate. I think a lot of it has to do with this country and the fact that this country is not more involved in terms of setting policy in that area.*

Lois Romano, "Donald Trump, Holding All The Cards: The Tower! The Team! The Money! The Future!"
***Washington Post*, 15 November 1984.**[15]

The international background to Trump's announcement that he wished to become an American negotiator with the Soviets on nuclear weapons was the development of the "New Cold War." Tension between the superpowers had been heightened in the early 1980s by the Soviet invasion of Afghanistan. It had intensified further after Ronald Reagan became president in January 1981 and distanced himself from the détente practised by his predecessors, seeing it as a cover for Soviet expansion and famously describing it as "what a farmer has with his turkey until Thanksgiving Day."[16] In the early 1980s, the escalation of the nuclear arms race between the superpowers had led to widespread anxiety and Trump seems to have shared these concerns. In future years, he would talk frequently about nuclear war, citing conversations with his uncle John G. Trump, a professor of engineering at the Massachusetts Institute of Technology, about the destruction that could be wrought by these weapons.

Trump's political adviser on this subject, Roy Cohn, had served as Senator Joseph McCarthy's chief counsel during the 1950s, playing a leading role in his anti-Communist witch hunt. Having established himself as one of New York's most formidable and feared lawyers, Cohn began representing Trump in the early 1970s, after the Department of Justice charged Trump and his father with refusing to rent to black tenants due to racial discrimination. He continued to serve as one of Trump's leading political confidants until his death from AIDS in 1986.[17]

Trump's desire to insert himself into the high politics of the Cold War was underpinned by his belief that his business practices could easily be applied to the diplomatic arena and that he could quickly and easily master the complexities of nuclear issues and missile technology.

His unwillingness to reveal any hint of his opinions on the subject publicly, claiming that it would undermine his negotiating position, will be familiar to those who followed his discussions of national security issues during the 2016 presidential campaign.

"In the event anything happens with respect to me. I wouldn't want to make my opinions public," TRUMP says. "I'd rather keep those thoughts to myself or save them for whoever else is chosen …it's something that somebody should do that knows how to negotiate and not the kind of representatives that I have seen in the past." He could learn about missiles, quickly, he says: "It would take an hour-and-a-half to learn everything there is to learn about missiles … I think I know most of it anyway. You're talking about just getting updated on a situation."

Trump advertisement in the *Washington Post, New York Times* and *Boston Globe*, 2 September 1987.

This full-page advertisement, which Trump paid $94,801 to run, caused a big stir on publication. It rehearses many of the themes that have dominated Trump's foreign policy rhetoric ever since. The US has a bad deal from its allies. Trump's argument is summed up in the words: "The world is laughing at America's politicians as we protect ships we don't own, carrying oil we don't need, destined for allies who won't help. Over the years, the Japanese, unimpeded by the huge costs of defending themselves (as long as the

United States will do it for free), have built a strong and vibrant economy with unprecedented surpluses." The result is American economic weakness.

The backdrop to Trump's intervention was the ongoing Iran–Iraq War. Following Iraqi attacks on Iranian shipping and refining facilities, Tehran responded in 1984 with assaults on neutral vessels. As a result, the United States expanded its naval presence in the region and provided support to its Arab allies in order to ensure the continued flow of oil, the majority of which still went to Europe and the Far East. As Iran stepped up its attacks over the succeeding years, the US undertook an operation in the summer of 1987 to reflag and escort Kuwaiti tankers, the largest naval convoy exercise of its kind since World War II. In July 1987, the Kuwaiti tanker *al Rekkah*, reflagged as the MV *Bridgeton*, was damaged by an Iranian mine while travelling under American naval escort, precipitating further hostility between the US and Iran. It also led to tension with America's allies in the Gulf. They were desperate to begin transporting oil again to their European and Asian markets and objected to the stringent US shipping regulations that were now required to transport the supplies through the heavily mined Persian Gulf, their only transportation outlet. American newspapers were also reporting that Kuwait and Saudi Arabia were refusing to provide landing facilities for American mine clearing helicopters, and that the Saudis were unwilling to use their own American supplied mine-sweeping ships, because they feared Iranian reprisals.[18]

Trump railed against the conduct of America's Arab allies but he was even more disgusted with US policy towards Japan, which depended on oil from the Middle East but relied on the United States to ensure its continued supply. Once again, there is no reference to the Soviet Union, perhaps less surprisingly, as the Cold War was now beginning to come to an end after the accession of Mikhail Gorbachev.

An open letter from Donald J. Trump on why America should stop paying to defend countries that can afford to defend themselves.

Donald John Trump

To the American people:

For decades, Japan and other nations have been taking advantage of the United States.

The saga continues unabated as we defend the Persian Gulf, an area of only marginal significance to the United States for its oil supplies, but one upon which Japan and others are almost totally dependent. Why are these nations not paying the United States for the human lives and billions of dollars we are losing to protect their interests? Saudi Arabia, a country whose very existence is in the hands of the United States, last week refused to allow us to use their mine sweepers (which are, sadly, far more advanced than ours) to police the Gulf. The world is laughing at America's politicians as we protect ships we don't own, carrying oil we don't need, destined for allies who won't help.

Over the years, the Japanese, unimpeded by the huge costs of defending themselves (as long as the United States will do it for free), have built a strong and vibrant economy with unprecedented surpluses. They have brilliantly managed to maintain a weak yen against a strong dollar. This, coupled with our monumental spending for their, and others, defence, has moved Japan to the forefront of world economies.

Now that the tides are turning and the yen is becoming strong against the dollar, the Japanese are openly complying and, in typical fashion, our politicians are reacting to these unjustified complaints.

It's time for us to end our vast deficits by making Japan, and others who can afford it, pay. Our world protection is worth hundreds of billions of dollars to these countries, and their stake in their protection is far greater than ours.

Make Japan, Saudi Arabia, and others pay for the protection we extend as allies. Let's help our farmers, our sick, our homeless by taking from some of the greatest profit machines ever created – machines created and nurtured by us. "Tax" these wealthy nations, not America. End our huge deficits, reduce our taxes, and let America's economy grow unencumbered by the cost of defending those who can easily afford to pay us for the defence of their freedom. Let's not let our great country be laughed at anymore.

Sincerely,

Donald J. Trump

Interview with Larry King, CNN, 2 September 1987.[19]

In this interview, Trump reiterates the themes of the *New York Times* advertisement, especially on the direct link between foreign policy failure and US economic weakness. If the United States was a corporation, he warns, it would be bankrupt. He elaborates somewhat on his critique of American allies, which he widens to include NATO and the (West) Germans, claiming that they are "ripping off the United States" and "laugh at us because of own stupidity and [that of our] leaders." In particular, Trump attacks the imbalances between US defence spending and that of the rest of the alliance. Overall, he believes that the United States should not be "the world's keeper." Trump also argues that "we don't have free trade right now" because Japan and Saudi Arabia distort the market. He claims that his foreign policy outlook is not motivated by his own financial interests, suggesting that he would personally benefit from Japan's fortunes if he decided to sell his properties to its wealthy citizens. In short, he believes that the United States may be "a great country ... but it's not going to continue being great for long" if it continues to defend counties that are "money machines," who would be "wiped off the face of the Earth if it weren't for America," without receiving sufficient tribute. This shows that similar remarks made in the 2016 election campaign were neither opportunistic nor did they come from nowhere.

Trump makes clear that he identifies as a Republican, but that he strongly disagrees with the foreign policy of the Reagan administration and, implicitly, that of all American administrations since the late 1940s. At this time, however, he again claims that he is not interested in running for the presidency, even though he admits he has agreed to speak at an event organised by Michael Dunbar, a conservative Republican in New Hampshire, who is seeking to draft Trump for a presidential campaign. When one caller suggests to Trump that the US should not force its allies to pay for protection and that it would be unconstitutional for the President, without Congressional approval no less, to turn the US army into a "mercenary force," Trump denies it would be unconstitutional and doubles down, claiming:

TRUMP: *If you're talking about taxing, I'm not talking about taxing. I think that people should make a contribution, and a major contribution – other countries – to this country for what we're doing to keep their freedom, and to keep them free, and to allow them to be free. And would you rather have that, or would you rather see this country go totally bust in another couple of years, because this country cannot afford to defend Japan and every other country in the world? It just cannot afford it.*

In response to a caller who asks him whether he favours a US–Canadian free trade agreement, Trump makes clear that he values the US alliance with Canada, stating that they have been "one hell of a good ally." He contrasts Canada with other countries, who he claims are bastions of anti-Americanism, who are receiving American largesse that should be going to support "our own people – the homeless, the sick, the poor, the farmer, who are really going through hell right now." When a caller suggests that Trump should put his money where his mouth is and support these groups, he deflects by claiming that federal assistance is required and that the government could do this if it received greater reimbursement from its allies.

TRUMP: *I don't want to single out Japan. I don't want to single out Saudi Arabia. But these are countries that people understand the kind of wealth we're talking about. And I will single them out, but there are many other countries, and – taking tremendous advantage of this, including NATO. If you look at the payments that we're making to NATO, they're totally disproportionate with everybody else's … If we had business ability in this country, we'd be making lots of profit – so-called surplus – profit. And that profit, that money, could be going to defend our – and I literally mean defend – our homeless, and our poor, and our sick, and our farmers. And that's where we ought to be spending the money. Not giving it to countries that don't give a damn for us to start off with.*

Fox Butterfield, "New Hampshire Speech Earns Praise for Trump," *New York Times*, 23 October 1987.[20]

In his speech in at the Portsmouth Rotary Club in New Hampshire on 22 October Trump once again blasts America's leaders for allowing the country to be "kicked around" by its free-loading allies. The *New York Times* claimed that Trump spoke before a larger audience than other American presidential candidates, including Senator Bob Dole, the Rev. Pat Robertson or Representative Jack Kemp, had previously drawn to the venue. Rejecting the idea that Trump was running for president, his executive assistant, Norma Foederer, told the *Times* that Trump was "genuinely concerned with the budget deficit and with America's declining position in the world and wanted to speak out." In his address, Trump dismisses the idea of a tax rise, instead repeating that "we should have these countries that are ripping us off pay off the $200 billion deficit." The speech is notable for its suggestion that the United States seize some Iranian oilfields in retaliation for Iran's attempts to intimidate American ships in the Persian Gulf. This is something that Trump had first mentioned in his 1980 interview with Rona Barrett and a theme that would resurface in a different form some 20 years later. Once again, Trump reiterates his favourite mantra that he wants someone in government "who is tough and knows how to negotiate."

Appearance on the *Phil Donahue Show*, WNBC, 16 December 1987.[21]

Having made his first intervention into foreign policy discussions on national television in 1980 to criticise the Democrat Jimmy Carter, Trump has now shown he is also willing to lambast the foreign policy of a Republican president, the party with which he, at least nominally, identifies at this time. During his presidency, Ronald Reagan had raised the nation's morale after the malaise that surrounded the end of the Carter presidency, but a series of scandals, most notably the Iran–Contra affair, had undermined the country's trust in his administration.

In this interview, Trump continues his attacks on America's partners or what he calls "our so-called allies," who he denounces as "a disaster for this country." He focuses particular attention on Tokyo again, reiterating that Japan and America's Middle East allies are "making billions and trillions of dollars while this country is going out and borrowing money from Japan in order to defend Japan." Again, he expresses resentment that the United States is responsible for keeping the sea lanes open from the Persian Gulf when other countries are more reliant on the Middle East as a source of oil. The connection between domestic and foreign policy is evident with his claim that increased domestic spending is dependent on the US receiving tribute from its allies. Once more, he also diverts the discussion when Donahue enquires about his own decision to build lavish projects in Manhattan rather than low-income houses elsewhere in New York by stating that it is America's overseas commitments that prevent the federal government from providing properties for its own citizens. Yet when Donahue raises the possibility that the United States should scale back its commitments and retreat from a major role in the Persian Gulf, Trump responds that the US does not need to choose between guns and butter.

TRUMP: *Before we committed [its naval forces to the Persian Gulf], we should have had Kuwait, Saudi Arabia, and a lot of*

other countries, and Japan, paying us a hell of a lot of money.
For us to lose, and there's no money that can justify this, but for
us to lose our men and to be spending billions and billions of
dollars, and we're not a wealthy nation, we are a country that's
losing 200 billion dollars a year. And we can't get farm aid
and we can't give welfare, we can't give this and that, and right
down the line – research on AIDs, and all of the problems –
and yet Japan is making hundreds of billions of dollars a year.
Now, again, I respect them. They have totally taken advantage
of this country. You can respect them, you can dislike them, you
can do whatever you want, but they are ripping off the United
States of America. Kuwait, Saudi Arabia – they're ripping
off this country and I don't like seeing it and it shouldn't
happen. …

If we got the money that we're entitled to from Japan, from
Kuwait, from Saudi Arabia from all of these other countries
that have taken such advantage of this great country of ours,
we wouldn't have to raise taxes. You could have all the Navies
you want and you could also have all the housing you want to
because that's the quinella – that's the big money Phil.

Interestingly, after the Donahue show, Trump received the
following letter from Richard Nixon:

December 21 1987

Dear Donald,

I did not see the programme, but Mrs Nixon told me that
you were great on the Donahue Show. As you can imagine,

she is an expert on politics and she predicts that whenever you decide to run for office you will be a winner!

With warm regards.

Sincerely,

Richard Nixon.[22]

It is not clear how Trump and Nixon were acquainted, although two Trump advisers, Roger Stone and the recently deceased Roy Cohn, had previously served under the former President.[23]

Appearance on the *Oprah Winfrey Show*, ABC, 25 April 1988.[24]

The context here is the 1988 presidential election to decide Ronald Reagan's successor. He rehearses all the old themes, but the language is becoming coarser, even macho: "you can respect somebody that's beating the hell out of you." Although Trump denies he is currently interested in running for president, he does tell Winfrey that "if it got so bad, I would never want to rule it out totally, because I really am tired of seeing what's happening with this country – how we're – how we're really making other people live like kings and we are not." He does promise, however, that if he ever did become president then "I can tell you one thing, this country would make one hell of a lot of money from those people that for 25 years have taken advantage." In the upcoming 1988 presidential election, he makes favourable reference to all the major candidates, although it is not clear that it is because he agrees with their positions rather than simply because it makes good business sense for him to stay on good terms with influential politicians.

TRUMP: *I'd make our allies, forgetting about the enemies, the enemies you can't talk to so easily, I'd make our allies pay their fair share. We're a debtor nation; something's going to happen over the next number of years with this country, because you can't keep going on losing $200 billion. And yet we – we let Japan come in and dump everything right into our markets and everything – it's not free trade. If you ever go to Japan right now, and try to sell something, forget about it, Oprah. Just forget about it. It's almost impossible. They don't have laws against it that they just make it impossible.*

They come over here, they sell their cars, their VCRs, they knock the hell out of our companies. And, hey, I have tremendous respect for the Japanese people. I mean, you can respect somebody that's beating the hell out of you. But they are beating the hell out of this country. Kuwait, they live like kings, the poorest person in Kuwait, they live like kings and yet they are not paying. We make it possible for them to sell their oil. Why aren't they paying us 25% of what they are making? It's a joke.

Appearance on *Late Night with David Letterman*, NBC, 10 November 1988.[25]

Appearing on David Letterman's prominent late night talk show, Trump here welcomes the victory of George H.W. Bush in the 1988 presidential election, which had occurred two days before. Trump's principal concern remains Japanese trade competition and that Japan, a country that he continues to regard as an economic rival more than a strategic ally, is not paying the US more to defend it.

LETTERMAN: *They kept saying that we're now existing in a false economy and that in a matter of months, weeks, years everything is going to topple down and this prosperity we have been seeming to enjoy will just evaporate now. Is that true and if so why?*

TRUMP: *I hate to say it but it could very well be true. Really we are living in very precarious times. If you look at what certain countries are doing to this country, such as Japan, I mean they've totally taking advantage of this country. The trade deficits we hear about, talking about the deficits, they come and they talk about free trade they dumped the cars and the VCRs and everything else. We defend Japan for virtually nothing, which is hard to believe, so when I see all that I get very nervous but I think George Bush is going to do a great job and I think he's gonna straighten out, hopefully, he's gonna straighten things out now.*

Polly Toynbee, "Towering Trump – The Tycoon is Big on Himself and it has Paid Handsomely, but What Can He Do For the People?" *Guardian*, 26 May 1988.[26]

Trump is addressing a foreign audience here, but the foreign policy themes are the same, especially with regard to

Iran and the link between America's bad deals abroad and its domestic economic weakness. Again, he pivots from Toynbee's enquiry into what he would do to address New York's housing crisis to his argument that America's domestic problems could be solved if it received larger indemnities from its allies. The emphasis on the lack of "respect" shown to the United States internationally is again striking. He describes the United States as a "second-rate economic power, a debtor nation." The United States was "getting kicked around" and becoming the "whipping post of its allies" because America's politicians were clueless. When Toynbee focuses on a concrete issue, US policy towards Iran, Trump responds:

TRUMP: *I'd be harsh on Iran. They've been beating us psychologically, making us look a bunch of fools. One bullet shot at one of our men or ships and I'd do a number on Kharg Island [at the time, the world's largest offshore crude oil terminal and Iran's principal sea port for the export of crude oil.] I'd go in and take it. Iran can't even beat Iraq, yet they push the United States around. It'd be good for the world to take them on.*

Interview with Shuichiro Ueyamaon, Japanese Television, 13 June 1988.[27]

This interview was hosted by Shuichiro Ueyama, a former employee of Sony, who had been involved in the development and marketing of Sony's Walkman, providing a stark reminder of Japan's mastery of the high technology market at this time. Once more, Trump pointedly claims that the "stupidity" of American politicians is to blame for economic backsliding in the United States. In particular, Trump asserts that nations like Japan are taking advantage of the United States by leveraging its assets (particularly defence cover and the ships used for oil transport in the Persian Gulf), without contributing. He claims that he believes good US–Japanese relations are important, because the two nations have shared interests, particularly the interlocking of their two economies. But he bluntly tells his interlocutor that Japan needs to pay more for its defence and that it was in their interests to do so, as America's decline would be to the detriment to Japan, too. It is not clear whether Trump is emphasising the economic or strategic disadvantages for Japan from a declining America. But what is again apparent is Trump's belief that the US and Japan do not mutually benefit from their alliance and that instead the Japanese exploit this relationship to prosper financially at America's expense. That they are allowed to do so, according to Trump, is "only a question of the stupidity of our policies."

TRUMP: *I think there is a great friendly relationship, and there always should be, between Japan and the United States because we have so many self-interests. I mean as an example, Japan, now is a major investor in the United States … But, I did criticise the Reagan administration and I criticised basically administrations of previous years because Japan has totally un-flanked our government. We defend Japan for*

*virtually nothing. Does that make sense? Here is Japan making billions and billions of dollars in profits and surplus. You know it is a difficult situation. Japan has very brilliantly, and I say brilliantly with great respect, very brilliantly made the United States look very foolish. And that is only a question of political leaders, that is only a question of the stupidity of our policies …
As an example, the Persian Gulf, we get ships to go into the Persian Gulf and out of the Persian Gulf and many of them go to Japan, as you know, you get much of your oil and fuel from the Persian Gulf. They come in and they go out and Japan doesn't pay anything and yet we're paying all the freight. Why isn't Japan contributing to this? These are just basic questions. I admire Japan for not doing it. I mean, anybody that can talk our not-so-intelligent politicians into a policy where we take oil out to go to Japan to fuel Japan's factories so they can make cars to sell in the United States and beat the hell out of our companies and they don't have to pay for that, I have to respect it.… Ultimately, [though], I am going to have to pay for it and so is everybody else. And, by the way, so is Japan because if the United States, [if] something negative should happen [to it], Japan is going to be in just as much trouble as the United States.*

Interview with Robert Lipsyte on "The 11th Hour," WNET, September 1989.[28]

This is an appearance on a local New York television channel, rather than the national audiences that we have hitherto seen Trump addressing. Once again, though,

Trump makes the link between domestic and foreign policy, arguing that the United States is providing Japan with free defence cover rather than rebuilding its own inner cities and providing free education to its citizens. Instead, he urges American leaders to slap high tariffs on Japanese goods entering the United States and ensure that Japan pays the US large sums for its defence commitments so that it can use its money to address problems at home. This is the essence of his grand strategy, as he tells the interviewer: "I like talking the big picture because the big picture is really what can solve the overall problem." His main concern is still Asia, but anxiety is also expressed about (West) Germany and Saudi Arabia. "You go look at Saudi Arabia and Kuwait and various other oil-producing countries," he says, "and you'll see lifestyle beyond belief. They have lifestyle because we give them their freedom and they give us nothing." Trump's zero sum attitude to trade relations is in evidence, as is his perennial critique that America's leaders are "fools." Interestingly, Trump claims in this interview to be a reader, but what he reads and what he has made of what he has read is not clear.

TRUMP: *There's no aggressiveness, there's no advocacy, and that's really the word. Everything's a compromise today. We don't want to anger Japan. They are friends. They are partners. Don't tax them. They're laughing at us! They think the United States is made up of a bunch of fools. They're laughing at us. Now they don't say it to our face because then we get insulted and then we do something about it. I will tell you, behind closed doors, they are laughing at the United States. They think we are the biggest fools, the dumbest people in the world because look at the way they're living. Look at the way we defend them, look at the way we opened up the Persian Gulf – most of the oil goes to Japan. We open up the Persian Gulf for Japan to get oil, for Saudi Arabia [and] Kuwait to make money. Why aren't they paying us for this? ... I want to tax Japan, I don't want to tax you. I want to tax West Germany, I want to tax Saudi Arabia. We keep them alive. If it weren't for us they wouldn't even be here, they wouldn't exist. I mean to think that Saudi Arabia would not allow us to use their minesweepers to police their own Persian Gulf is beyond me. I want to tax Saudi Arabia for the job we do in keeping them alive. They wouldn't be here for 20 minutes if we ever said "you're on your own baby."*

Interview with Glenn Plaskin, *Playboy*, March 1990.[29]

By the time this interview took place, the world had changed radically. The Berlin Wall had come down. The Communist regimes in Eastern Europe has collapsed. The Cold War had completely ended. Trump's world view and rhetoric, however, has not changed. He once again lambasts America's leaders for allowing its allies to "literally out-egotise this country," stresses the importance of "respect," bewails the imbalances of trade, especially with Japan, and toys with the idea of the presidency. Trump also gives his impressions of the Soviet Union, having travelled to Moscow in 1987 to investigate building a hotel there.

While that did not work out, Trump had begun to take an interest in Mikhail Gorbachev's attempts to reform the country and even claimed to have read the Soviet leader's 1987 book, *Perestroika*. When Gorbachev visited the US in late 1988 to speak at the UN and for meetings with Reagan and his successor Bush, Trump even invited Gorbachev to dine privately at Trump Tower. Gorbachev actually agreed to this proposal, although constraints on the Soviet leader's time meant the meeting with Trump was cancelled.[30] By the time that Trump sat down with *Playboy*, however, Gorbachev had presided over the disintegration of Soviet dominance in Eastern Europe and Trump had soured on his leadership. Trump suggested that the Soviet "system is a disaster," although as usual he rated their leaders as "tougher and smarter than our representatives." Nevertheless, Trump informed *Playboy* that he foresaw revolution and the fall of Gorbachev, who did indeed lose power a year later. He contrasts the international perception of Gorbachev as a "wonderful leader" with the domestic chaos then engulfing his country and Trump's view that he was "destroying the Soviet Union." Significantly, his complaint against Gorbachev is that he was not showing "a firm enough hand." By contrast, the Chinese regime at Tiananmen Square "were vicious, they were horrible, but they put it down with strength" and this demonstrated "the power of strength." This is in line with Trump's general demand for "toughness," which he defines as "being mentally capable of winning battles against an opponent and doing it with a smile. Tough is winning systematically."

Despite the end of the Cold War, he calls for an increase in America's own defence spending and suggests that the country was still suffering from a lack of international respect that went back to the Carter administration and its failed attempt to rescue American hostages in Iran. Trump is now starting to distance himself from President George H.W. Bush, scorning his talk of a "kinder, gentler America" and calling for the businessman Ross Perot, who would launch a third party campaign for the presidency in 1992, to be put in charge of American foreign policy negotiations. For his own part, he claims that his hypothetical administration would "believe very strongly in military strength" and would have a "huge military arsenal, perfect it, understand it." Somewhat ironically given the concerns about his ties to Moscow today, Trump claims "he wouldn't trust anyone; he wouldn't trust the Russians; he wouldn't trust our allies."

* * *

When asked what the first action that President Trump would take upon assuming office, he declares that he would "throw a tax on every Mercedes-Benz rolling into this country and on all Japanese products, and we'd have wonderful allies again." And indeed this very much echoes the threats that Trump made in his interviews with foreign press organisations after he won the presidency.

While this may be Trump's short-term priority, his long-term concern continues to be the prospect of nuclear conflict, which he claims to think about often:

TRUMP: *I've always thought about the issue of nuclear war; it's a very important element in my thought process. It's the ultimate, the ultimate catastrophe, the biggest problem this world has, and nobody's focusing on the nuts and bolts of it … Too many countries have nuclear weapons; nobody knows where they're all pointed, what button it takes to launch them. The bomb Harry Truman dropped on Hiroshima was a toy next to today's.*

Interview with Larry King, CNN, 18 April 1990.[31]

Once again, Trump laments that the United States is defending Japan, West Germany and Saudi Arabia while they prosper economically. Moreover, he repeats a prediction that he first made in his March interview with *Playboy* that Gorbachev will soon be forced from power and that the Soviet Union was on the verge of collapse.

TRUMP: *I predicted a long while ago, and I got a lot of real heat on it, that Gorbachev would be, essentially, that Russia was going to break up … now I'm saying it much more strongly. I mean now a lot of people are saying that but I did an interview for all places* Playboy *and this was really done about six months ago and I said I think that Gorbachev is going to be out and Russia is going to disintegrate and now I say it much more strongly because it looks like that's happening.*

Note on the 1990s

During the 1990s, Trump appears to have intervened less frequently in American foreign policy debates. This may be a product of US victory in the Cold War and its resulting "unipolar moment," or the fact that Trump was in the midst of a high-profile divorce and was mired in personal financial problems after a number of his companies filed for bankruptcy protection in the early 1990s. Although Trump had recovered his financial position by the mid-1990s, he did not take an active role in the 1996 presidential campaign or seem to have made any major foreign policy pronouncements around that time. By 1999–2000, however, he is back on the old themes. Two things, however, have changed. First, the principal competitor in Asia, and globally, is no longer Japan, which had just experienced its "lost decade," but China. Secondly, Trump expresses a disdain for nation-building, at that time a swipe against the liberal interventionism of Bill Clinton rather than the neoconservatism of George W. Bush.

Donald J. Trump, "Donald Trump on the Embargo and Casinos," *Miami Herald*, **25 June 1999.**[32]

In 1999, Trump was entertaining the idea of running for president on the Reform party ticket and this article was an attempt to reach out to Cuban–American voters in Florida, which pundits correctly predicted would be a crucial swing state in the 2000 presidential election. Trump would follow up this article by delivering a speech in Miami in

November 1999, in which he doubled down on his hard-line position. On that occasion, he declared "if the embargo is not continued, then the Bay of Pigs and all the people who died or were injured and those who are living monuments of it will be hurt by this government a second time."[33] Donald Trump's strong ideological statements appear in direct contrast to the unsentimental realism with which he is often associated. Yet Trump's rhetoric does not appear, in fact, to reflect the reality of his personal, business conduct. He has since been accused of exploring business opportunities in Cuba in 1998, which would have broken the embargo in place on the island. On Thursday, 29 September 2016, in the midst of the 2016 presidential campaign, *Newsweek* published a front-page report charging Trump Hotels & Casino Reports with paying around $68,000 to a consulting firm that would provide Trump with advance access to the Cuban market if the US decided to loosen trade sanctions, which President Bill Clinton was rumoured to then be exploring.[34] Yet in 1999, Trump had claimed:

TRUMP: *Yes, the embargo is costly. If I formed a joint venture with European partners, I would make millions of dollars. But I'd rather lose those millions than lose my self-respect. I would rather take a financial hit than become a financial backer of one of the world's most-brutal dictators, a man who was once willing to aid in the destruction of my country. To me the embargo question is no question at all. Of course, we should keep the embargo in place. We should keep it until Castro is gone.*

Maureen Dowd, "Liberties; Trump L'Oeil Tease," *New York Times*, 19 September 1999.[35]

Trump's comments to Dowd again illustrate his emphasis on the need for decisive leadership. At the time, Hillary Clinton was conducting a four-day tour through Upstate New York as she explored the possibility of running for one of the state's Senate seats. Trump would also point to Churchill when discussing leadership with Larry King in his 8 October 1999 interview, stating that Britain's wartime prime minister was an "unbelievable leader;" despite being "born with a speech impediment, he had all sorts of problems, he certainly wasn't a handsome man, and, yet, he was a great leader." It is unclear whether Britain's current Prime Minister, Theresa May, was aware of Trump's admiration for Churchill when she sent the President-elect a Christmas letter on 29 December that referenced Churchill's historic address to the American people on Christmas Eve 1941, shortly after US entrance into World War II, and called for the 'special relationship' to continue to be inspired by the "most famous British-American."[36]

"The concept of the listening tour is ridiculous. People want ideas. Do you think Winston Churchill, when he was stopping Hitler, went around listening?"

Interview with Larry King, CNN, 8 October 1999.[37]

This interview is Trump's first major foreign policy statement for almost ten years. The previous decade had seen massive shifts in the global balance. The United States remained the uncontested master of the world system, and had intervened militarily in Bosnia in 1995 and then in Kosovo in 1999. Trump, though, picks up more or less where he left off at the start of the decade, attacking Germany, Saudi Arabia and Japan for "ripping [off]" the United States, creating trade imbalances, and aiming a broadside at France, referring to it as "the worst team player I've ever seen in my life." He continues to argue that the US could institute reforms at home, such as funding health care and reducing taxes, if it introduced higher tariffs on foreign goods and charged its allies more for defending them. He claims not to be an isolationist. This statement is partly motivated by the desire to distance himself from Patrick Buchanan, a former candidate for the Republican nomination in 1992 and 1996, and then a contestant for the Reform party nomination. Buchanan had recently published a book which claimed that Nazi Germany was not a military threat to the United States after 1940 and Trump joined in the general denouncement, ridiculing Buchanan's suggestion that "Hitler would have never attacked us, Hitler would have gone a different direction."[38] However, while Trump dismisses isolationism, he does state that "if other countries are not going to treat you fairly, Larry, I think that those countries should be – they should suffer the consequences," although it is not clear what those ramifications would be. He also predicts that when the economy fails "NAFTA is going to look like a disaster," a position that he would continuously reference during the 2016 presidential campaign.

The interview is most notable for Trump's scepticism about the NATO campaign in Kosovo. Trump's language is vague and unclear, but he seems to be suggesting that he would have preferred the introduction of a large ground force to the use of air power. What is striking about this is that Trump's military doctrine normally seems to revolve around the use of air power and surgical strikes rather than ground forces; on this occasion, however, he appears to be arguing the opposite.

Trump would later state in his 2000 book, *The America We Deserve*, that he was, in fact, "delighted that there was a happy ending in Kosovo" and that he credited this to "excellent air power."[39] As his shifting response to the Libyan intervention in 2011 would later illustrate, Trump's positions could fluctuate both during and after a military campaign.

TRUMP: *Well, I would have done it a little bit differently. And I know this would sound terrible. But look at the havoc that they have wreaked in Kosovo. I mean, we could say we lost very few people. Of course, we had airplanes 75,000 feet up in the air dropping bombs. But, look at what we've done to that land and to those people and the deaths that we've caused. Now, they haven't been caused with us and the allies because we were way up in the air in planes. But, at some point, you had to put troops in so not everybody could go over the borders and everything else, and a lot of people agree with that. Now, would people have been killed? Perhaps, perhaps more. But, at least ultimately, you would have had far fewer deaths. And you wouldn't have had the havoc and the terror that you've got right now. So, you know, I don't know if they consider that a success because I can't consider it a success … They bombed the hell out of a country, out of a whole area, everyone is fleeing in every different way, and nobody knows what's happening, and the deaths are going on by the thousands.*

Donald Trump (with Dave Shiflett), *The America We Deserve* (2000), pp. 111–91.

This book is co-written, in effect probably ghost-written, by Dave Shiflett and lacks the immediacy of Trump's interview statements.[40] Nonetheless, it reflects his broad sentiments and reprises many old themes. Trump continues to assail American leaders for their naivety, suggesting that the US acts as an "older brother to regimes that are playing us for suckers." He is dismissive of foreign policy "experts," who he ridicules for failing to predict the end of the Cold War. However, he does express admiration for Henry Kissinger and references Kissinger's thesis, which he claims that the veteran foreign policy statesman told him personally, that "American foreign policy is always shifting back and forth between two extremes – either starry eyed idealism or brooding isolationism."

While the 1990s has come to be known as America's "holiday from history," when the US was unrivalled as the world's supreme power, the book strikes a more foreboding tone. It suggests that "storm clouds [are] brewing." Economic disaster continues to be Trump's most pressing concern. New elements are trade anxieties about China ("our biggest long-term challenge"), which henceforth replaces Japan in his demonology. But now emerging as a second pressing concern is terrorism. Strikingly, given that it was written before 11 September 2001, the book mentions Osama bin Laden by name as a threat to the United States. Islamist extremists had already been responsible for a 1993 bombing on the World Trade Center and bin Laden had orchestrated the 1998 United States embassy bombings in Kenya. Trump's fear that the next attack on the American homeland would make that "look like kids playing with firecrackers," echoed the worst nightmares then being expressed by Bill Clinton's administration.[41] He again refers to the influence of his uncle, MIT Professor John G. Trump, for instigating his nightmares about nuclear war.

Significantly, given Trump's scepticism about NATO during the 2016 presidential election campaign, he states that "we can pull our troops out of Europe" and "protect Europe with our nuclear arsenal and use those funds for schools" in the United States.

CHAPTER 3
APPRENTICE: PROTECTING THE NATION, 2001–14

At the outset of the twenty-first century, both the United States *and* Donald Trump had shown that predictions about their demise had been greatly exaggerated. Despite fears in the late 1980s that the United States was in decline, it entered the new century as the world's sole superpower. And Trump, after falling heavily into debt in the early 1990s, was once again New York's most flamboyant and showiest real estate developer. He was less active in US foreign policy debates in the 1990s, distracted, perhaps, by his financial and personal difficulties, but possibly also because the United States was "beating" everybody else in all categories, especially the economy and military power. Having declined to run for president in 1992, 1996 or 2000, in the latter case as a Reform party candidate, Trump's focus was once again on his business empire.

On 11 September 2001, however, the Al Qaeda terrorist attack on New York's Twin Towers struck at the heart of America's financial capital and Trump's own world. It was the largest terrorist attack in US history, killing nearly 3,000 people and destroying a symbol of America's economic power and prosperity. For Trump, who had built a number of New York's tallest and most opulent skyscrapers, the blow hit close to home. His first public responses were relatively measured. He suggested that if he was president then the response would be "very very tough." His sense that people knew "at least approximately the group of people that did this" is not expanded upon, but Islamist extremists had already attacked the World Trade Center before in 1993 and in Trump's 2000 book *The America We Deserve* had stressed the threat from Islamic fundamentalism and Osama bin Laden. After George W. Bush's administration responded by going after bin Laden and Al Qaeda, their attention turned to Iraq. On the first anniversary of 9/11, Trump expressed measured support for the looming conflict with Iraq but voiced his wish that the United States had removed the threat from Saddam Hussein after the first Gulf War (1990–91). Once the war started, Trump was not a vocal opponent of it, but nor was he a cheerleader. As the war soured, Trump expressed compassion not only for the American casualties, but also for the civilian Iraqi victims of the conflict.

During the first decade of the century, Trump's fame massively increased as he emerged as a reality TV star, on the mega hit show, *The Apprentice*, which spawned an international franchise. Consequently, Trump's own celebrity status was more secure than ever. He had added a media fiefdom to his real estate empire, providing him with a new base from which to launch a presidential campaign if he decided to do so.

At the same time, by the end of George W. Bush's presidency, the position of the United States as the pre-eminent global power was once again being questioned. The US remained engaged in a "War on Terror" and its forces were engulfed in conflicts in Afghanistan and Iraq. The American economy was in the throes of the "Great Recession" and China had now emerged as America's principal global competitor. In 2008, the political commentator Fareed Zakaria wrote of a "Post-American world" and the "end of Pax Americana." To illustrate his argument, Zakaria recalled that, during the 1980s, when he would visit India, where he grew up, people were fascinated by the United States and the figure that particularly intrigued them was Donald Trump. As Zakaria noted, Trump was "the very symbol of the United States – brassy, rich, and modern," and he "symbolised the feeling that if you wanted to find the biggest and largest anything, you had to look to America." Yet Zakaria observed that India now had dozens of its own businessman who were "wealthier than the Donald." For Zakaria, this epitomised a wider global trend that he referred to as the "rise of the rest," signalling an end to America's "unipolar moment" and a global power shift towards countries of the non-Western world.

Zakaria was adamant that this should not unsettle Americans. Instead, he urged them to recognise that the "post-American world" was actually a product of "American ideas and actions" and a result of "trends that have created an international climate of unprecedented peace and prosperity."[1] Yet, as Zakaria acknowledged, many Americans did not see things like he did. They had become suspicious of free trade, economic openness and immigration. What was not yet clear, though, was that none other than Donald Trump would present himself as their champion.

Interview with Alan Marcus, WWOR-TV, 11 September 2001.[2]

MARCUS: *In the year 2000, Donald you considered running for president. If you had done that, and if you had been successful, what do you think you'd be doing right now?*

TRUMP: *Well I'd be taking a very, very tough line, Alan. I mean you know most people feel they know at least approximately the group of people that did this and where they are but boy would you have to take a hard line on this. This just can't be tolerated and it's got to be very, very stern. This is as you and I were discussing before, Alan, this was probably worse than Pearl Harbor. Many more people are dead.*

Appearance on *The Howard Stern Show*, WXRK, 11 September 2002.[3]

This is one of Donald Trump's numerous appearances on *The Howard Stern Show*, which took place as the United States was girding for war with Saddam Hussein, and attempting to put together an international coalition against him. Trump's tepid expression of support for the invasion of Iraq in this interview would become a subject of controversy during the 2016 presidential campaign when he claimed to have opposed the conflict from before it began. Just before the excerpt begins, Trump and Stern had discussed 9/11 and the moment the planes hit the Twin Towers.

TRUMP: *I'm not sure things are any tougher. They sound tougher but I'm not sure they are tougher in terms of security. And you know it's also nice to know your enemies … you like to know who they are at least. We really don't know the enemy.*

STERN: *They're scoping around somewhere and you feel like a sitting duck.*

TRUMP: *But we have an idea who the enemy is and a lot of times the politicians don't wanna tell you that.*

STERN: *Are you for invading Iraq?*

TRUMP: *Yeah … I guess so. I wish the first time it was done correctly.*

The conversation turns to rebuilding the World Trade Center and choosing a Memorial.

TRUMP: ... *if we don't rebuild something really substantial and create lots of jobs and everything else in addition to a great memorial then they've won – at least they've won that part of the battle* ...

Appearance on *Your World With Neil Cavuto*, Fox News, 28 January 2003.[4]

Trump's critique here of the administration's open telegraphing of military plans is reminiscent of his earlier opposition to discussing his nuclear negotiation plans and his later vow not to announce his plan against ISIS in public. "Whatever happened to the days of Douglas MacArthur," he asks, "He would go and attack. He wouldn't talk." Trump finds "the concept of a newscaster talking about the [possible invasion] routes, just ... ridiculous." For him "the point is either you do it or you don't do it." If you do not do anything, he demands, then one should not even talk about it, presumably because it reduces credibility. He repeats this point a number of times during the interview. Interestingly, Trump does not seem to see any difference between secret operational plans and a grand strategy which needs to be owned and explained.

TRUMP: *When I watch Dan Rather explaining how we are going to be attacking, where we're going to attack, what routes we're taking, what kind of planes we're using, how to stop them, how to stop us, it is a little bit disconcerting. I've never seen this, where newscasters are telling you how – telling the enemy how we're going about it, we have just found out this and that. It is ridiculous.*

Appearance on *Your World With Neil Cavuto*, Fox News, 21 March 2003.[5]

This interview, which took place a day after the invasion of Iraq began, includes a belligerent swipe against France who he says "never liked" the US "except when we were bailing them out," and the hope that the invasion would be a "tremendously successful campaign." Mainly, however, it is notable for Donald Trump's concern about the sensibility of America's allies ("there are a lot of countries right now that aren't too fond of us"), a point not made in any truculent sense. Striking is also his muted phrasing of the WMD issue ("it will be very interesting to see what kind of weapons they find"). To this extent, Donald Trump did not at the outset quite share the general enthusiasm for the war and its claimed basis, which was Iraq's possession of weapons of mass destruction.

TRUMP: *But certainly we're going to have to work on our public relations because there's no question there are a lot of countries right now that aren't too fond of us. I think that can be solved and probably pretty quickly. The main thing is to get the war over with and just make it a tremendously successful campaign and it will be very interesting to see what kind of weapons they find.*

Appearance on Scarborough Country, MSNBC, 11 September 2003.[6]

On the second anniversary of the 9/11 attacks, and six months after the commencement of the war in Iraq, Trump makes a brief appearance on Joe Scarborough's MSNBC show and says that he would "not necessarily" have invaded Iraq. This comment was made after the invasion had been completed and the insurgency was already beginning to take its toll on the US occupation forces, but some time before popular, political and press opinion had shifted against the war. It underlines further Trump's early scepticism about the whole project.

TRUMP: ... *It wasn't a mistake to fight terrorism and fight it hard, and I guess maybe if I had to do it, I would have fought terrorism but not necessarily Iraq.*

Donald J. Trump, "Donald Trump: How I'd Run The Country (Better)," *Esquire*, August 2004.[7]

At the height of the Iraqi insurgency, and the travails of American power there, Trump reprises and enlarges upon his existing, post-Kosovo, scepticism about "nation-building." He doubts that Iraq will ever be a "wonderful democracy" where the losers accept the judgement of the ballot box. Instead, he predicts that "two minutes after we leave, there's going to be a revolution," during which power will be seized by "the meanest, toughest, smartest, most vicious guy." He repeats his concern about Iraqi casualties. He also laments the fact that "countries we are protecting [OPEC] are screwing us on oil prices."

TRUMP: *What was the purpose of this whole thing? Hundreds and hundreds of young people killed. And what about the people coming back with no arms and legs? Not to mention the other side. All those Iraqi kids who've been blown to pieces. And it turns out that all of the reasons for the war were blatantly wrong. All this for nothing!*

Interview with Wolf Blitzer on CNN's "Late Edition," 21 March 2004.[8]

This interview took place in the context of the steep decline of American world standing after the invasion of Iraq, the general sense within the United States that its Middle Eastern policy was bogged down and the upcoming presidential election in November 2004. Trump states that the United States "is not a very popular country right now," indeed he argues that "maybe it shouldn't be such a popular country. I mean we're not running a popularity contest." Interestingly Trump states that "in many cases I probably identify more as a Democrat," citing the economy as an example.

TRUMP: *Well, I will say this. And again, I like the president very much, but I think that this – this is not a very popular country right now. It's interesting, New York City is trying to get the Olympics, and I'm all for it. But I think it's tough to give New York City the Olympics right now, because I think a lot of countries that would have voted for us strongly right after September 11th maybe don't like us so much anymore.*

Interview with David Hochman, *Playboy*, October 2004.[9]

This interview, which took place as the US slipped ever deeper into the mire in Iraq and the presidential election loomed in November 2004, is notable in several ways. First, it continues the old critique of America's allies, especially Saudi Arabia. Secondly, it notes the absence of weapons of mass destruction in Iraq. Thirdly, it once again laments not merely American but Iraqi casualties, including "beautiful Iraqi children being killed and maimed, walking around with no legs and no arms." Fourthly, it expresses further scepticism about nation-building in the Arab world, especially Iraq which can never hope to enjoy "normal democratic government," predicting that "as soon as we leave the country will be taken over by the next dictator." He makes similar prognostications about Afghanistan. Fifthly, the interview indicates that Trump's favoured form of military engagement is not ground war but the surgical use of air power, or as he puts it: "spot hits instead of sending in the troops." During the interview, Trump in effect endorses John Kerry for President, describing him as "a great guy, a very smart guy." Most strikingly of all, the interview expresses renewed concern about the new generation of weapons of mass destruction, which "are too powerful" and he laments that "access to the weapons is getting too easy."

TRUMP: *[speaking of his late uncle, the MIT scientist, Dr John G. Trump] He was a brilliant scientist, and he would tell me weapons are getting so powerful today that humanity is in tremendous trouble. This was 25 years ago, but he was right. The world is rocky, and some terrible things are going to happen. That's why I lead the life I do. I enjoy it. I know life is fragile, and if the world looks like this a hundred years from now, we'll either be very lucky or have found unbelievably good leaders somewhere down the line.*

Gaby Wood, "Donald Trump: The Interview," *Observer*, 7 January 2007.[10]

In an interview with the British left-leaning weekly the *Observer*, Trump declares that his priority, if he ever became president, would be to "try and solve the problems in the Middle East.'" While emphasising his belief that he was capable of resolving the region's problems, he is vague as to details. It is not clear whether he is talking about solving the problems in Iraq, where US troops were engaged in the "Surge," or the Arab–Israeli conflict, which had again escalated the previous summer when the Iranian-backed, Lebanese-based Hezbollah terrorist organisation kidnapped and killed Israeli soldiers, precipitating a 34-day conflict between the two sides. Trump's conviction that, as an accomplished "dealmaker" he could bring peace to the Middle East, is clearly stated.

TRUMP: *[in response to the question of what he would do if he were President] First, I'd try and solve the problems in the Middle East – that could be solved. It's sad what's happening, but let's go on to another subject. [When challenged as to what his solution might look like he replied]. Well, it can be solved. Everything can be solved if you have talent.*

Interview with Larry King, CNN, 15 April 2009.[11]

This lengthy and important interview took place during the honeymoon of Barack Obama's election as President of the United States. Despite having endorsed the unsuccessful Republican candidate, John McCain, Trump gives the new Democratic President a fair wind, especially on foreign policy. He is almost star-struck. Trump says that Obama is a "wonderful personality, a good speaker, somebody that people trust" and that "he's trying to rebuild our reputation throughout the world," which had been damaged by the outgoing Bush administration, "a total disaster, a total catastrophe" in his view. The new President is "really doing a nice job in terms of representation of this country." For the rest, Trump simply rehearses his old arguments about the link between American foreign policy and US domestic decline. "We are fighting wars in Iraq and yet we are not taking care of New Orleans" Trump complains, saying that the money used on protecting the world would be better spent on "protecting ourselves." Towards the end, Trump takes aim again at OPEC: "They'll just start raising the price of oil again and destroy the economy." Trump also goes a step further, attacking Saudi Arabia not just for free-riding under the American security umbrella, but also for being the real sponsors of the 9/11 attacks. It was Saudis, he notes, who "had a lot more to do" with the attack on the World Trade Center, to which the US had foolishly responded by attacking Iraq.

TRUMP: *[when asked for his view of Barack Obama he responds] Well, I really like him. I think that he's working very hard. He's trying to rebuild our reputation throughout the world. I mean, we really have lost a lot of reputation in the world. The previous administration was a total disaster, a total catastrophe.... The world looks at us differently than they used to. And I think he's trying to restore our reputation within the world. And he was handed a pretty bad deck of cards. I mean, he was given a pretty tough situation.*[12]

Extract from Donald Trump (with Meredith McIver),
Think Like a Champion: An Informal Education in Business and Life.

What is striking about this extract is Trump's continuing regard for President Obama, who has a "a very good chance" of being a "great" leader, and his attempts to address the international image of the United States, which he says is "hated" across the world. It is clear from these remarks that at this time, Trump set a lot of store by the opinions of the outside world. Later he would attack the President for apologising to the Muslim world.

TRUMP: *After 9/11, this country received a lot of compassion from countries and people around the world. Within a short amount of time, however, we were hated. How did that happen? We had no dialogue with other countries because they just plain hated us. What's different today is that we have a new chance, a new beginning. The world is excited about Barack Obama and the new United States. Let's keep it that way.*

Appearance on *Late Show with David Letterman*, CBS, 11 March 2010.[13]

The context here is mid-term disenchantment with the Obama administration. Trump may also already have been exploring a possible presidential run in 2012. All the old familiar themes are rehearsed again: OPEC is "ripping off" the United States, China's "underselling and selling without taxes" and "in 10 years China will surpass us." OPEC, he says, operates like a cartel "setting prices" which "screw the customer," that is the United States. Making a direct pitch for the presidency on the basis of his business experience, Trump says "we should use our great business people to negotiate, not some diplomat that knows nothing about business."

TRUMP: *Well, the way I look at it. If OPEC is going to keep ripping us off with their oil prices. And if China is gonna keep underselling and selling without taxes or anything else. This country has a lot of problems. I don't see recovery. Really, I don't see greatness unless we do something about China and some others and OPEC ... In 10 years, if it keeps going at this pace, in 10 years China will surpass us. And that's pretty pathetic.*

Appearance on the *Joy Behar Show*, CNN, 8 December 2010.[14]

By this point Trump has turned decisively against President Obama, launching a critique in which foreign policy and domestic grievances are inextricably intertwined. Despite being "very hawkish," Trump believes that the Iraq War is "one where we should never have been in the first place, and which had created the Harvard of Terrorism" there. He renews his attack on Saudi Arabia, albeit more obliquely this time when he says that "it certainly wasn't Iraq" which attacked the Twin Towers. He again dismisses nation-building as a will of the wisp which is diverting resources from the economic reconstruction of the United States. "I don't want to build roads in Iraq," he announces, "I want to build roads in New Jersey." His objection to Obama is that "the world does not respect us" and that "China is eating our lunch." Trump also targets Mexico and the effect that the transfer of jobs is having on the Midwest. There is the standard attack on OPEC, which is "11 guys sitting round a table and just dictating the price of oil," and that he says only "the right leadership" can stop by forcing the price down to $40 a barrel, in his view the level required for US economic recovery. He suggests once again that the country needs someone with business experience, "somebody that knew a little bit about the art of the deal."

TRUMP: *One of the problems that I think this country has with taxes is that a lot of the people disagree with where the money's being spent. I mean I'm a very hawkish person, as you probably know. I mean, I'm a great hawk. Yet we're in two wars and certainly one where we should have never been in the first place. And people say, well, wait a minute, they're raising my taxes. I don't want to build roads in Iraq. I want to build roads in New Jersey. I want to build roads in Iowa. I want to build roads where – like in this country. I don't want to build schools in someplace when in St. Louis we can't build our own schools. [On President George W. Bush] I thought he was a disaster. I thought he didn't do a good job. I thought he did – he had an opportunity after the World Trade Center to really make this country into a popular place. You know, the world loved us for the first time. They used to fear us. Then they used to dislike us. And then they loved us for a very brief period of time. And we had a chance to really translate that into something good. And he just blew it.*

Remarks at the Conservative Political Action Committee (CPAC) Conference, 10 February 2011.[15]

Here Donald Trump both repeats standard lines about China, Mexico and OPEC "ripping" the United States and showing a lack of "respect" for it. He claims not to be opposed to "free trade" as such, arguing that "we don't have free trade" and "we don't have fair trade" because the Chinese "manipulate their currency," by keeping it "artificially low." Trump says that the United States needs someone who will "call out OPEC" by telling them "that price better get lower fast." In effect, what Trump envisages is a kind of unilateral international de-cartelisation by the United States. Towards the end of the interview Trump laments that "Germany is buying the New York stock exchange," asking whether this is April Fools' day. He also sets out how he would deal with the Somali pirates. Just "give me one good admiral and a couple of ships," he says to applause, and "we'd blast them out of the water so fast."

TRUMP: *The United States has become a whipping post for the rest of the world. The world is treating us without respect. They are not treating us properly. America – [applause] America today is missing quality leadership and foreign countries have quickly realised this. It is for this reason that the United States is becoming the laughing stock of the world … I deal with people from China, with people from Mexico. They cannot believe what they are getting away with. I have said on numerous occasions that countries like China, like India, South Korea, Mexico and the OPEC nations view our leaders as weak and ineffective and have repeatedly taken advantage of them to the tune of hundreds of billions of dollars a year …*

We don't have free trade. We don't have free trade. We don't have fair trade and I am a fair trade believer.

I love open markets, but not when China is manipulating their currency.

"From the Desk of Donald Trump," Video Posted by The Trump Organisation, Uploaded on 28 February 2011.[16]

This statement is very much an outlier with regard to Donald Trump's general view on liberal intervention, but it does show the extent to which humanitarian arguments have traction with him. The context was the outbreak of a popular revolt against the long-time Libyan dictator Moammar Gaddafi. Rejecting gradualist solutions through trade embargoes and other measures, Trump demands that "we should do it on a humanitarian basis, immediately go to Libya, immediately go into Libya" and "knock this guy out very quickly." Perhaps mindful of the failure of the Iraq intervention, he claims that "ultimately the people will appreciate it." He adds that "they should pay us back," reimbursing the US with oil, thus reconciling his seemingly humanitarian rhetoric with the need to avoid providing security for free. Trump's hawkishness here may be related to Gaddafi's near-iconic villainous status in the United States in the 1980s, when Trump's world view was being formed. In keeping with Trump's general view on the use of military force, which heavily emphasises air power over ground troops, he calls for the operation be conducted "surgically."

TRUMP: *I can't believe what our country is doing. Gaddafi in Libya is killing thousands of people. Nobody knows how bad it is and we're sitting around, we have soldiers all over the Middle East and we're not bringing the men to stop this horrible carnage. And that's what it is, it's a carnage. You talk about all of the things that have happened in history, this could be one of the worst. Now we should go in. We should stop this guy which would be very easy and very quick. We could do it surgically, stop him from doing it and save these lives. This is absolute nuts. We don't want to get involved and you're going to end up with something like you've never seen before. Now ultimately the people will appreciate it. They're going to end up taking over the country eventually but the people will appreciate it and they should pay us back.*

Interview on *Piers Morgan Tonight*, CNN, 28 March 2011.[17]

In mid-March 2011, NATO finally intervened on behalf of the rebels in Libya and Trump almost immediately began to have second thoughts. A prolonged air campaign resulted, during which Trump gave this interview. He also asks to know why the Arab League "aren't paying for this." Trump, however, does not yet abandon his belief that intervention and the removal of the Libyan dictator is necessary. Indeed, he says that intervening without making regime change an explicit object, which the president has been doing to avoid Congressional challenges and other objections under international law, "makes no sense whatsoever." "If you don't get rid of Gadaffi," he reiterates, "it's a major, major black eye for this country." At the same time, Trump insists on the complexity of the situation and expresses understanding for President Obama's predicament in this regard.

TRUMP: *[on President Obama] I think he's trying hard. He's under a lot of stress. It's not an easy situation. I do really want to know who these people we're fighting for, who they are. They call them the rebels like they're these wonderful guys. But I hear they are aligned with Iran. I hear they may be aligned with Al Qaeda. To be honest, wouldn't that be really very, very sad if we're bombing all of these tanks, killing all of these people, one way or the other, and Iran ends up taking over Libya?*

Interview on *The O'Reilly Factor*, Fox News, 30 March 2011.[18]

This interview seems to be one of the first sustained, televised engagements by Donald Trump with the issue of illegal immigration, which he sees as a question of nationhood and national security. "Either you have a country or you don't," he says, "You either have a line and a boundary or you don't." He calls for a militarisation of the border with Mexico ("you put soldiers on that line"), the germ of his plan for a wall that caused such controversy during the 2016 presidential election campaign. This interview also appears to signal the escalation of his feud with Islam generally, when he says "there is a Muslim problem" in the world, "you just have to turn on your television set." The pattern of engagement with both issues is remarkably similar. On the one hand, Trump says that illegal

Mexican immigrants are "selling drugs all over the place" and "killing people all over the place." On the other hand, Trump also acknowledges that "some great productive people" have come in, for whom there would have to be a "case by case" decision. On the one hand, Trump links Muslims to terrorism generally, saying that "I don't notice Swedish people knocking down the World Trade Center," and claiming that the Qur'an is full of "tremendous hatred." On the other hand, Trump also concedes that "you have fabulous Muslims. They're smart, they're industrious."

TRUMP: *[when asked about his stance on illegal immigration]. Well, you either have a country or you don't. You either have a line and a boundary or you don't. Something has to be done ... you put soldiers on that line. [When asked why mainstream Muslims do not speak out more forcefully against terror] Well, there is something out there that brings a level of hostility that I have never seen in any religion. I mean, you can say what you want about the Qur'an. You can say what you want, but there's something there. There is tremendous hatred and tremendous hatred of us. I look at Iraq. I was watching the other day, you know, we have spent all this money and all those lives in Iraq. They hate us. They hate us. They can't get rid of us fast enough.*

Interview on *The O'Reilly Factor*, Fox News, 31 March 2011.[19]

This long discussion is largely a rehash of all the usual themes about China, OPEC, free-riding allies, the human cost of the Iraq War and the need to secure Iraqi oil for the United States. The interview is notable in some respects, however. First, because it identifies Britain as a country that has "helped" the United States and must be "taken care" of, one of the few allies about whom he has been willing to make favourable statements. He also seems to praise France for taking the lead in Libya. Secondly, the interview shows his ambivalence about the Libyan intervention. On the one hand, Trump supports "stopping that kind of a slaughter." On the other hand, "the problem is where do you stop," showing his concern with the selectivity and potentially open-ended nature of the interventionist project. Moreover, Trump worries about "the so-called rebels" who are linked to Iran and Al Qaeda. Thirdly, Trump gives a clear indication that he will "do what he has to do" to prevent Iran from acquiring a nuclear weapon, presumably a military strike. Finally, Trump renews his assault on President Obama: "our weak president that kisses everybody's ass" but "is in more wars than I have ever seen." Trump asks why he is seen as a "warmonger" while Obama is a man "who got the Nobel Peace Prize" and yet "every time I look he is going into another war."

TRUMP: *I've never said this before. This is the first on your show. Good luck with it. Run with it. In the old days when you had wars, you win, right? You win. To the victor belonged the spoils. So when we go to Iraq, we spend $1.4 trillion so far and thousands of lives are lost, right? And not to mention all* *the poor guys and gals with one arm and no arm and all the facts, right?....You stay and protect the oil and you take the oil and you take whatever is necessary for them and you take what's necessary for us and we pay our self back $1.5 trillion or more. We take care of Britain, we take care of other countries that helped us and we don't be so stupid [when asked about the Iranian nuclear programme]. I wouldn't let them have a nuke. [When asked how he would stop it, he answers] I would do what I had to do.*

Interview on *The O'Reilly Factor*, Fox News, 1 April 2011.[20]

Trump takes aim at Pakistan for supporting the Taliban in Afghanistan. He believes that the main problem for the US in the War on Terror lies in Pakistan rather than in Afghanistan itself. Trump therefore demands that Washington issue an ultimatum to Pakistan to surrender Osama bin Laden. If it did, he predicts, then "he'll be standing on the White House doorstep very quickly." Trump also briefly sets out his general view of the use of military power. "I don't believe too much in the soldier concept" he says referring to the idea of a ground attack on Al Qaeda sanctuaries, "other than I believe in air power ... You can knock hell out of them without losing soldiers and losing lives." He repeats his scepticism about nation-building. "I want to build our country," Trump says, "You know in Afghanistan they build a school. They blow up the school. They blow up the road. We then start all over again." This activism comes at the expense of the United States, Trump claims, saying that "in New Orleans and in Alabama, we can't build schools."

TRUMP: *If Osama bin Laden is in Pakistan, why are we paying them hundreds of billions of dollars a year? Now what I would say, "Don't get scared. I want to get along, fellows. I love you. Let's go have a drink. But you're not getting money. We want Osama bin Laden. Because if you don't give us Osama bin Laden, we're just not giving you hundreds of billions of dollars."*

Interview with George Stephanopoulos, ABC News, 18 April 2011.[21]

This long interview took place while Trump was considering a bid for the presidency in 2012. He rehearses the usual grievances about trade, now firmly directed against China rather than Japan, and his opposition to the Iraq War. He repeats his demand that the United States seize Iraqi oil to pay for the costs of the war ("to the victor belong the spoils") and to prevent the Iranians from seizing it. Trump undertakes not merely to use the money to "take care of" the families of soldiers in Iraq, to distribute it to Iraq itself and to "reimburse our partners," presumably powers like the United Kingdom. He once again slams OPEC as "12 guys around a table" who say "let's screw the United States." Trump once again makes a direct link between foreign weakness and domestic decline, something which has always been part of his bedrock beliefs, and is also vital to his potential electoral appeal. "The reason they're trying to cut health care," he claims, "is because China is going to make $300 million profit this year off the United States and steal a lot of our jobs." The cause of the misery, he argues, is "because we have poor leadership." The solution, Trump argues, lies in the articulation of national will by a great leader.

TRUMP: *Look. I'm going to look 'em in the eye and say, "Fellas, you've had your fun. Your fun is over." I look at what's going on with our country. We're like a third world nation....*

We are going to do things with them that are very, very simple. They're going to understand how the game is played. And one other thing. They wouldn't be there if it weren't for us. We protect them. We keep those countries going and we get nothing for it.

Interview with Xinhua (Official Chinese News Agency), 3 May 2011.[22]

In this remarkable interview, Trump claims that he has "read hundreds of books about China over the decades." He also claimed to "know the Chinese," with whom he had "made a lot of money." On this basis, Trump believes that he "understands the Chinese mind." When asked to list some of the intellectual influences on his view of China, Trump apparently named 20 volumes off the top of his head, including Henry Kissinger's *On*

China, Jung Chang's *Mao: The Untold Story,* Peter Navarro's *The Coming China Wars,* Stefan Halper's *The Beijing Consensus,* Gavin Menzies' *1421* and Amy Chua's *Battle Hymn of the Tiger Mother.* Of course, one should not deduce from this list, which is a suspiciously round figure of 20, that Trump has read all these books or necessarily agrees with them. It is, however, an established fact that Donald Trump proactively reached out to at least one of the authors on the list to discuss China policy well before the 2016 election. It is also the case that one of the authors on this list, Peter Navarro, has been appointed to an important position in the new administration.

This was also reported in *Asian Correspondent,* on 7 June 2011: *The Xinhua interview was immediately pulled offline by Communist censors (purportedly because it mentioned banned books such as* Mao: The Untold Story *by Jung Chang and Richard McGregor's* The Party). *But Trump's "Best China Books" list nonetheless went viral across the web. Everyone from book critics to Sinophiles were now abuzz not about Trump's trade war with the Chinese, but the LITERATURE that had led him to making such extreme policy decisions.*[23]

Interview on *The O'Reilly Factor,* Fox News, 12 December 2011.[24]

In this interview, Donald Trump resumes his attack on the usual suspects. "Everybody is beating us ... and they are sapping our wealth." Notably, he sets out a hierarchy of challenges, of which he rates China "number one." Trump also works through in general terms what a trade confrontation with China would look like, claiming that the United States has "all the cards and chips." He says that he would impose a "25 percent tax" on all Chinese items imported into the US, which would "put China out of business." Trump argues that the central factor, as always, is the connection made between domestic and foreign policy, which in Trump's view lies at the heart of the US economic malaise. "We have to take care of our country from the inside," he says, "and we have to fight the people from the outside." Because China "manipulate their currency," he says "manufacturing … is going to China and other places instead of having it in Alabama and Iowa." He concludes by expressing the hope that "we would start producing our own products," perhaps the opening shot in his later presidential campaign to "bring back" lost manufacturing jobs to the United States.

TRUMP: *[on being asked by O'Reilly whose "butt" he would kick first if president]* I would say China number one. I would say OPEC probably number two. The OPEC nations. What they are doing with oil is unbelievable; over $100 a barrel in a bad economy. They monopolise what they are doing with oil. It's absolutely – anywhere else it would be illegal … *[when O'Reilly responds that China might retaliate by selling its holdings of American debt, Trump replies that]* We have all of the power. All of the chips are on our side. The trillion, it's actually $1.1 trillion that they have, forget it, that's peanuts *compared to the overall economy. Now, what I would say very strongly, you don't start behaving, 25 percent tax on every item you sell in this country. Twenty-five percent right now. By the way, based on what they are doing, it should be 41 percent.... It will put China out of business. We have all the cards and chips. If that ever happened, they would have a depression the likes of which you have never seen. They cannot play that game. We can.*

Interview on *State of the Union with Candy Crowley*, CNN, 17 April 2011.[25]

Here Trump elaborates his critique of the OPEC cartel and renews his attack on President Obama. "Obama is not the right messenger," he says. "We are not a respected nation any more. The world is laughing at us." He demands that the United States tell OPEC: "Fellows, that price is going down." Trump argues that "we can't be the policeman for the world," a swipe here not so much at humanitarian intervention as the provision of security cover without recompense. Once again, he demands that the United States reimburse itself from Iraqi oil: "When you have a war and you win that nation's yours." The rest of the interview is devoted to the standard critique of China which is "stealing our jobs and taking our money." The result is that the United States has become a "Third World Nation."

TRUMP: *Look at Libya. Look at this mess. We go in; we don't go in; he shouldn't be removed; we don't want to remove him; we don't want to touch him, but he should be removed. Nobody knows what they're doing on Gaddafi.*

Then we're back into rebels – oh gee, whiz, maybe we can't, because they're backed by Iran. You know, if somebody said, "What would be your theory or what would you do in terms of Libya," I'd do one thing. Either I go in and take the oil or I don't go in at all. We can't be the policeman for the world.

Interview on *Piers Morgan Tonight*, CNN, 4 January 2012.[26]

This interview sheds light on how Donald Trump came by his later campaign slogan "Make America Great," to which he proposes adding the word "again."

TRUMP: *I have millions of people that want me to run. They want me to run as an independent. They want me to run as anything. They formed a party out in Texas, Make America Great. And I said, boy, what a great name for a party. That is a great name for a party, because that's what it's all about, Make America Great. I guess I'd add the word again. But I don't think you can do that.*

Interview on *Piers Morgan Live*, CNN, 13 June 2013.[27]

What is striking about this interview, especially in the light of Trump's reaction to more recent revelations about the role of Wikileaks and the Russians in assisting his election, is the hostility shown towards the whistleblower Edward Snowden. Trump considers him "bad news."

TRUMP: *[on Snowden] I think he's bad news. I've watched him and he's having a good time. And of all places he goes to Hong Kong for protection. That in itself is a little bit interesting because that's not a place where actually he should get that kind of protection but it looks like they are going to protect him ... As far as, you know, privacy, certainly we want the privacy. Now people are saying that this is national security and it really depends on how far they're going and that will come out, but we do want privacy. We also want national security.*

Interview on *Piers Morgan Live*, CNN, 13 September 2013.[28]

The immediate context here is President Obama's decision not to attack President Assad's regime in Syria, despite the fact that it had just openly crossed a "red line" established by his administration on the use of chemical weapons, because Russia had offered a compromise solution. This important interview gives us an insight into Donald Trump's view of Putin, which is initially ambivalent. He laments the fact that President Obama is being "outplayed" over Syria which is "making us look very bad as a country," and expresses grudging admiration for Putin who though "not nice at all" was "about as tough as you're going to get." Trump also criticises Obama for going back over his "red line" on Syria. Trump stresses the importance of "surprise" rather than giving away one's military strategy in advance. At the end he reverts to his view that "we cannot be the policeman of the world" and that "we have problems in this country that we have to solve before we start helping people that hate us." Finally, Trump returns to his old refrain about keeping one's strategic cards close to one's chest.

TRUMP: *It all began when we he used the term red line, he's going to draw a line in the sand essentially and don't cross. That they crossed but he didn't do anything and then it became very late, and he decides to go back to Congress, and Congress is having fits over it, and it looks like he wasn't going to even come close to getting the vote and he started looking very, very ineffective. And then, of course the letter or the editorial that Putin wrote at the* New York Times *was amazing. It was just amazing. He said so much. And he said it in a very nice way but it wasn't really nice at all. It was tough, about as tough as you're going to get. And Obama is having a very, very hard time competing.*

Interview on *Piers Morgan Live*, CNN, 10 October 2013.[29]

This interview is a standard attack on the usual targets who are "taking advantage" of the United States. China and OPEC are the "two chief abusers," with the Chinese "manipulating their currency" and "taxing our products when we send them." He links the continuation of social security programmes such as Medicare, Medicaid to a fresh start in international trade policy and thus for the US economy. "If we don't have the right leadership," Trump argues in a clear pitch for the presidency, "we will never have a great economy again and we frankly will not be a great country again."

TRUMP: *You have to take jobs away from other countries, China, India, all of these countries, they're taking our jobs … We've made it so good for Mexico, what they're doing to us is unbelievable. You've got to take the jobs, you got to make the economy strong. And you know what, when you make the economy strong: Medicare, Medicaid, Social Security, all of the things that are in trouble, they won't be in trouble anymore…. If you can create a great economy, we don't have to worry about Social Security and Medicare and Medicaid, all things that are good things, we don't have to worry about them again.*

Interview with Thomas Roberts, MSNBC, 9 November 2013.[30]

This interview, which takes place while Trump is in Moscow for the Miss Universe Pageant, shows the extent to which Trump has begun to relate positively to Putin, with whom he says he "has a relationship," though it is not clear whether the two have ever met in person. The

Russian leader, he argues has done "a very brilliant job in terms of what he represents and who he is representing," which is rather two-edged praise, perhaps intentionally so. The key thing for Trump is that Putin "has really eaten our president's lunch" in Syria. These statements are clearly an attempt to diminish President Obama rather than exalting Vladimir Putin as such. The concrete "relationship" referred to here appears to pertain to his business presence in Moscow. During the 2016 campaign, Trump would deny ever meeting Putin.[31] Trump also repeats his usual assaults on "China and lots of other places that just rip us" and "are really taking advantage of our country and our people."

TRUMP: *[Roberts asks whether Trump has a relationship with Putin] I do have a relationship and I can tell you that he's very interested in what we're doing here today [the 2013 Miss Universe contest]. He's probably very interested in what you and I are saying today and I'm sure he's going to be seeing it in some form. But I do have a relationship with him and I think it's very interesting to see what happened. I mean look he's done a very brilliant job in terms of what he represents and who he's representing. If you look at what he's done with Syria if you look at so many of the different things he has really eaten our presidents lunch, let's not kid ourselves. He's done an amazing job. He's put himself really, as you know, a lot of people would say, he's put himself at the forefront of the world as a leader in a short period of time.*

Interview on *Piers Morgan Live*, CNN,
11 December 2013.[32]

This interview simply rehearses the familiar attacks on China. What is striking, though, is his willingness to do business with the Chinese on an individual level and the similarity of his comments about them to those made about Japanese businesses in the *The Art of the Deal* in the late 1980s.[33] It shows that the key to Trump's view of the world is his assessment of whether a given country is treating the United States with the "respect" it is owed.

TRUMP: *[of the Chinese] They want to be in my buildings, they're not blaming me for saying it and I have many friends at the top levels of China and they can't believe they're getting away with it. So, I would agree with you, I blame the politicians, I blame the leadership of this country, they're taking our jobs.*

Donald Trump at the 2014 Conservative Political
Action (CSPAN) Conference, 6 March 2014.[34]

The context here is the Russian occupation of the Crimea, part of the sovereign state of Ukraine, which had taken place three weeks earlier. Remarkably, Trump does not condemn this flagrant breach of international law and threat to European peace and security. Instead, he praises President Putin and the "great" reception he himself recently received in Moscow, on the occasion of his 2013

"Miss Universe" contest. Once again, the main purpose of his remarks seems to be to denigrate President Obama's weak "leadership," as one might expect when speaking to a Conservative Political Action Conference at that time, including instances where the President has failed to stand up to Russia. All the same, the sense that Trump considers Putin somehow a kindred spirit is palpable throughout Trump's rhetoric. The rest of the speech rehashes familiar themes about China, the need to rebuild the United States rather than other nations and the call to "take the oil" because "to the victor belongs the spoil." Trump also bewails how the world has "no respect for our leader and … no respect any longer for our great country." He claims that the Chinese, who "love" him and want his buildings, ties and other merchandise, will "respect you if you are smart" and tough. Trump concludes by vowing, in an echo of his campaign slogan, "to make America great again."

TRUMP: *We have so many problems and we have so little leadership. So little leadership. And it's all about the leadership … I was in Moscow a couple of months ago, I own the Miss Universe Pageant and they treated me so great. Putin even sent me a beautiful present with a beautiful note. I spoke to all of his people. You look at what he's doing with President Obama, he's like toying with him. So he has the Olympics, the day after the Olympics he starts with Ukraine. The day after. How smart? He didn't want to do it during the Olympics, boom, the day after. So our athletes leave, we all leave and the day after. You know, when he goes in and takes Crimea, he's taking the heart and soul, because that's where all the money is. I was surprised. I heard that the other day, they were saying most of the wealth comes right from that area. That's the area with the wealth. So that means the rest of Ukraine will fall and it's predicted to fall fairly quickly … I want to make the country so strong. We can do it. We're sitting on top of something that's so amazing, such incredible wealth. And the way you solve all of these problems, tremendous wealth and job production, strength in our military, not weaken, we've weakened our military. They want to cut our military. We listen to Putin about what we're going to get. No, we don't want you to use those missiles, oh, we won't order them. It's hard to believe. The bottom line very simple, make America strong again, make America great again. We have such unbelievable potential. We have to use it. We need the right leaders. Thank you all very much.*

CHAPTER 4

CANDIDATE AND PRESIDENT-ELECT, 2015–17

In the 2016 presidential election campaign, foreign policy remained central to Donald Trump's message, which was pushed out in an avalanche of tweets, television and radio appearances, speeches and debates. There are far too many of these to reprint either in full or in representative selection. Some were long and obviously "vetted" policy statements, where Trump was speaking from a script not necessarily his own. Most were short blasts in campaign mode, when the candidate was firing more than usually from the hip. If we step back from the fray, however, and attempt to listen above the "noise," it is clear that the underlying themes he addressed in those turbulent months were more or less the same ones that he had been elaborating over the past three-and-a-half decades since his first documented foreign policy pronouncement in 1980.

During this period, Trump had laid out a crude, but distinctive and coherent foreign policy position to which he returned time and again, especially in the context of presidential election campaigns. The United States, Trump claimed, was being "ripped off" and disrespected internationally. Its supposed friends, Japan, West Germany and Saudi Arabia, were "taking advantage" of the US over trade and pocketing their military protection by the United States through NATO and other alliances without giving anything meaningful in return. The economic problems besetting the United States were thus products of the nation's bad "deals" internationally. What was striking about this critique was that it focused more closely on America's friends than its avowed enemies, and its complete lack of interest in the Cold War contest, which was at its height when Trump first entered the fray in 1980, and was a battle which the United States was widely perceived to be losing.

As is often the case with the politically active, there was ambiguity and contradictions. On the one hand, Trump generally identified himself as what political scientists call a "realist," that is someone who eschews sentiment, "nation-building," humanitarian intervention and the provision of public goods, for the "hard" realities of power politics.[1] He seemed to have no qualms about doing business in Russia under the (late) Communists or the current Putin regime. Trump also described himself as a "hawk," determined to restore America's military might. On the other hand, Trump, at least rhetorically, claimed that he refused to deal with the Castro regime for ideological reasons; he initially supported intervention against Gaddafi in Libya, at least partly on "humanitarian" grounds; he objected to the Iraq War not only as a strategic error but also on account of the casualties inflicted on the Iraqi population; he acknowledged the talent and decency even of illegal immigrants; and he was much more concerned about the threat of nuclear war than is widely realised, particularly when compared to his apparent indifference to nuclear proliferation during the 2016 presidential campaign.

The record also shows a sometimes surprising Trump. Few who saw him in action in 2015–16 would expect him to show much compassion with the Iraqi civilian victims of the American invasion, but he did so on several occasions. Nobody who saw him ride roughshod over the sensibilities of foreigners on the campaign trail would imagine him to have been concerned with the global image of the United States, but he apparently worried that America's international reputation had been damaged during President George W. Bush's presidency and, at first, genuinely seems to have welcomed President Barack Obama's attempts to improve what he viewed as America's tarnished world standing. In terms of military strategy, the burden of Trump's remarks over time has been to support the standoff use of airpower, but to be very cautious about the lengthy deployment of large numbers of ground troops.

There were some important shifts in Trump's positions in the past 20 years, in particular the replacement of Japan by China in his trade demonology, and the ever greater salience of terrorism and domestic security after 2001. Trade and security concerns fused in Trump's increasing preoccupation with immigration, which enabled him to target both radical Islam and the economic threat posed by Mexico. Never much concerned with the Soviet threat, Trump's view of Putin shifted from annoyance to admiration of the Russian leader, partly because he had humiliated the "weak" and "ineffective" President Obama, but mainly because Trump related to Putin's "tough" stance, especially on terrorism. In general, though, there was remarkable consistency to Trump's foreign political thinking over time, accentuated as we have seen by its expression in a rather limited vocabulary.

These themes were coarsened, flattened and simplified, even beyond the usual low standards of a political campaign, during the 2015–16 electoral season, and garnished with some opportunist positioning. Nonetheless, they were still recognisably the same messages that Trump had been communicating since he first made his views on foreign policy known decades earlier. The critique of NATO, which caused such consternation in the US national security elite and capitals on the other side of the Atlantic, had been voiced in outline long before. Trump's ferocious attacks on China and other trade rivals were of a piece with what he had been saying for decades. Even the demand to seize Iraqi oil – "to the victor the spoils" – which hit the headlines during the campaign, had been made several times before and originated in a more general plan first advanced more than 20 years ago, to seize the oil reserves of the Middle East, or at the very least to break the monopoly of OPEC. And, above all, there remained the constant lampooning of America's leaders as "foolish" and "stupid" for allowing the country to be exploited by wily foreigners.

Between his election and inauguration, Donald Trump appeared to row back on a number of domestic issues, in particular on "Obamacare," but there was not even a hint of any shift on foreign policy. On the contrary, the President-elect doubled-down on his rhetoric against China. His acceptance of a congratulatory call from Taiwan's President Tsai Ing-wen led Chinese officials to protest that Trump was violating the "One China" policy – a diplomatic acknowledgment of China's position that Beijing is the sole Chinese government and a pledge that the US had adhered to since the establishment of formal Sino–US diplomatic ties in 1979. Trump responded to protests with a tweet that accused China of hypocrisy. It criticised Beijing for not asking the US "if it was OK" to devalue their currency to make it tougher for American businesses to sell goods there, for heavily taxing US exports to China and for expanding its military presence in the South China Sea.[2] Trump also signalled a change in US policy over Syria, where he advocated supporting Russia and Bashar al-Assad in the belief that they would fight ISIS more effectively. Even more important than what he said, is what the President-elect did *not* say. Some very weak pro-NATO noises aside, Trump made no effort whatsoever to reassure his European allies. Indeed, his interviews with

The Times of London and Germany's *Bild* only served to increase their fears. The question-mark over the security of the continent loomed larger than ever. None of this should have come as any surprise to anyone familiar with Trump's pronouncements over more than three decades.

After the initial shock of Donald Trump's election started to wear off, the usual reading of tea leaves about the new administration began in earnest. His appointments and nominations were scrutinised for clues as to what a Trump presidency would mean for the world.

Of course, it was true on one level that President Trump, like all other presidents, was filling positions taking both ideology and party management into account, for example, balancing the appointment of Steve Bannon, a leading light of the "alt-right," as chief strategist, with that of Reince Priebus, a stalwart of the Republican establishment, as chief of staff. Something similar was visible in the foreign policy sphere where the two most important choices pointed in fundamentally different directions on one of the critical issues facing the administration, namely Russia. On the one hand, President Trump's secretary of state, Rex Tillerson, had extensive business connections in Russia prior to assuming office, and was awarded the Russian "Order of Friendship" in person by President Putin in 2012. One of President Trump's first appointments, his initial National Security Advisor (NSA), General Mike Flynn, had argued for a common front with Moscow over Syria (although he had expressed reservations about Russia in other respects). On the other hand,

Mike Pompeo, his pick for CIA Director, was deeply suspicious of President Putin's ambitions in the Middle East and strongly critical of the threat he poses to NATO. And Trump's Defense Secretary, Ret. Gen. James Mattis, had taken a strong stance against Putin, suggesting in his confirmation hearing that "he is trying to break the North Atlantic alliance" and that there were "a decreasing number of areas where we can engage cooperatively and an increasing number of areas where we're going to have to confront Russia."[3]

This fudge offered few clues as to the future policy of the United States. But it seemed unlikely that Donald Trump's lack of detailed knowledge of world affairs, and his rocky relationship with the party's national security experts, would increase the influence of the professionals in the State Department. Nor was it right to expect the new President to fall back on Mike Pence, his vice-president, as the inexperienced George W. Bush did with Dick Cheney. President Trump knew his own mind, especially on major strategic challenges, and had made it clear that he would pay little heed to the Republican foreign policy establishment or party grandees. His estimation of Mike Pence became clear when he almost forgot to thank him during his victory speech. Moreover, the two men have very different world views, a fact that was demonstrated most publicly during the second presidential debate. Trump dismissed Pence's position that the US ought to meet Russia's "provocations" in Syria with a forceful response, simply declaring "he and I haven't spoken, and he and I disagree."[4]

Besides, Trump, who had spoken openly of possible candidate appointments as "finalists" in the manner of his TV-show *The Apprentice*, could fire as quickly as he hires. There was no guarantee that anybody who was in his cabinet in January 2017 would be there a year or two later (except the vice-president who could not be fired, but who could, of course, be side-lined and potentially removed from the ticket for 2020).

The speculation appeared pointless in another respect. It was already clear what kind of animal President Trump was. His world view was fully-formed; his temperament was well-known. Behaviourally, President Trump was the silverback gorilla, the narcissist peacock, the alpha male, the bull in the china shop. Politically, he was a Bourbon who had learned and forgotten nothing over the past three decades. It seemed unlikely that you could teach an old dog like him new tricks. The leopard would not change his spots.

After Trump's election victory, political analysts were left wondering what impact his style and temperament would have on world affairs. During the campaign, he had shown himself to be misogynistic, vindictive, thin-skinned, xenophobic and unafraid to trample on the feelings of veterans or the bereaved. Would Trump's personality translate internationally into an instinctive rapport with other "outspoken" figures such as Vladimir Putin in Russia, President Erdoğan of Turkey or President Duterte of the Philippines? And in the event of disagreement between them and Trump, was there a risk of vituperation on both sides in ways that were not compatible with the traditional dignity of the American presidency? The risks posed by President Trump's temperament were exacerbated by his modus operandi. His propensity to tweet from the hip at all hours threatened to derail the inter-agency process, by which presidential statements are vetted and risked precipitating a crisis. The world now appeared at some risk of the President being tricked into hasty action by provocateurs or worse still Trump's Twitter account being hacked by an outside power and used to disseminate false messages. More generally, given Trump's serious anger management issues, there were concerns that a clever adversary would get under his skin, provoke outbursts and either make a laughing stock of the greatest power on earth or precipitate a confrontation.

Futhermore, there were fears that Trump's Presidency would lead to the "Berlusconification" of global politics, and result in international diplomacy becoming extended reality TV events, at least in so far as they related to the United States. More serious, was the possibility that his antics would empower and encourage a coarsening of the discourse between states and about world problems. Here the contrast with President Trump's immediate predecessors, Presidents Bush and especially Obama, whatever one thought of their policies, could not have been more sharp.

Other aspects of Trump's temperament and conduct also elicited concern. First, despite all his rhetoric of deal-making in business and real estate, where his experience was considerable, and he had often shown a capacity to compromise, Trump's pre-presidential rhetoric suggested that he had a very limited and belligerent idea of what constituted a successful diplomatic negotiation. Rejecting notions of "win-win," a political "deal" seemed to involve the imposition of his will on the other side. As a consequence he cleaved to an essentially mercantilist view of world trade in which – say – Mexico's gain was America's loss.

Secondly, Trump had expressed immense confidence in his own judgement, even in areas in which he had no technical expertise. He claimed in 1984, at the height of fears about the threat of nuclear war between the United States and the Soviet Union, that "it would take an hour and a half to learn everything there is to learn about missiles. I think I know most of it anyway."[5] Of course, all politics in a democratic state in the end boils down to a decision by the man or woman legitimated to take it; to a judgement rather than the simple application of expertise and rightly so. All the same, the underlying insouciance which Trump had shown towards the question of technical knowledge and his disregard for the need for deeper understanding of complex problems did not bode well for the future.

Thirdly, Trump had long championed a particularly intuitive style of decision making. He had said in the past people "are surprised by how quickly I make big decisions, but I've learned to trust my instincts and not to overthink things."[6] Of course, international politics often require speedy decisions, but what would President Trump's instincts mean now that he had the proverbial finger on the button? This issue was highlighted during the election campaign by a whole phalanx of Republican national security experts, none of whom thought he should be entrusted with the nuclear codes.

It was expected that there could be little reliance placed on the restraining force of his advisers, or of the bureaucracy in the State and Defence Departments. When asked during the election campaign to identify those he consulted most often on foreign affairs, he replied that "I'm speaking with myself, number one, because I have a very good brain and I've said a lot of things."[7] The foreign policy "team" he had produced during the campaign was the weakest and most obscure that anybody had ever seen in living memory. This attitude continued to characterise his conduct after he won the presidency and before he was inaugurated. He defended his decision to only receive intelligence briefings on a weekly basis, rather than daily as is customary, by declaring: "I'm, like, a smart person."[8] His resolution that he should only receive intelligence briefings if something had dramatically changed suggested that his world view was pretty well established and unlikely to alter unless something seismic occured.

As far as policy was concerned, it was essential to distinguish between rhetoric recently adopted to wage the election campaign, and long-standing positions that Trump had been espousing for more than thirty years. Many of Trump's most noxious positions were of relatively recent origin and, at least prior to the 2011 "birther" conspiracy campaign about President Obama's citizenship, had not previously been central to his public, political interjections. His campaign rhetoric threatened to cause substantial economic and cultural rebalancing, and some pretty brutal measures against terrorism and illegal immigration, but there were constitutional bulwarks that would likely limit how far this could go. The bad news for the rest of world was that the beliefs most threatening to the international system, were the ones that Trump most deeply held, and which he was in the best position to implement.

Globally, Trump might have appeared at first glance as if he was advocating a number of positions that have been prevalent in the Republican Party for some time. During the campaign, Trump declared that the United Nations was "not a friend to freedom" and it appeared unlikely that he would pay any heed to the organisation whatsoever.[9] This position was in keeping with a strain of thought long evident in the Republican Party and represented most forcefully by former Ambassador to the UN, John Bolton, who advised Mr Trump during the campaign and once famously declared that if the UN building in New York "lost ten stories, it wouldn't make a bit of difference."[10] Trump's skepticism on climate change was reflected in the appointment of Myron Ebell, who does not believe in global warming, to lead the transition team for the Environmental Protection Agency. The choice of Rick Perry, the former Governor of Texas and enthusiastic driller, as Energy Secretary was in sync with a position espoused by a number of Congressional Republicans. Trump had indicated that he would press ahead with fracking and drilling on all fronts, in order to guarantee energy security for the United States. In this, it could be argued he was operationalising the "Drill, baby drill!" slogan championed at the 2008 Republican National Convention by incoming RNC Chairman, Michael Steele, and later popularised by vice-presidential nominee Sarah Palin.

But it would be a mistake to see Trump's pre-presidential foreign policy positions as establishment Republican ones. For in almost every significant area of international policy, Trump's pre-presidential stance represented a fundamental departure, not only from his Democratic predecessor and recent Republican incumbents, but from the entire bipartisan consensus that has existed in US foreign policy since the end of World War II.

As we have seen, the key to understanding Donald Trump is his quest for the restoration of US national "greatness," which he sees as having been lost, *not only by* the retreats and compromises of the Obama years *and* the interventionism of George W. Bush, but as a consequence of the national security strategy that successive US presidents have followed since the early years of the Cold War. Economics is central to Trump's vision, but it is not the deciding factor. To be sure, re-establishing economic strength is important. It will enable the United States to sustain Trump's otherwise prohibitively expensive plans, especially the proposed huge infrastructural programme, his tax cuts and the massive increase in military spending. The new President believes not in international, but national capitalism, based on construction and manufacturing, rather than trade and finance. One may not share President Trump's vision of restoring American prosperity and pride through civilian work creation, motorways and armaments, but it is a coherent programme. Unlike free-traders and globalisers, who see all boats rising on the tide of a growing world economy, Trump takes a much darker and mercantilist view of a zero-sum game. It is not the economy, it is national greatness, stupid!

Threatening US greatness, so the Trumpian critique claims, are not only America's enemies but America's friends. Politically, the main threat is radical Islam, which he says the Obama administration refused to call by its name, and has been aggravated by a costly and failed "nation-building" project in Iraq. Economically, it was China and Mexico, who were accused of effectively stealing US manufacturing jobs after the reduction of tariff barriers. Not much better, though, are America's principal European and Asian allies, particularly Japan and Germany, who are free-riding under the US defence umbrella and taking unfair advantage on trade. These are all positions which Trump has consistently elaborated in some detail over a long period of time.

During the campaign, Trump served notice that he would either abandon or ignore the institutions of international governance which the United States has done so much to establish. He was adamant that he would abrogate the Trans-Pacific Partnership, "re-negotiate" the North Atlantic Free Trade Area and probably drop the Transatlantic Trade and Investment Partnership – a trade deal being negotiated between the US and the European Union – assuming it was not already killed off on the other side of the Atlantic. This economic readjustment would be a precursor to a more far-reaching revamp of the geopolitical order.

Trump intimated that he would pay little heed to global human rights initiatives, whether it be the banning of torture or collective action to help Syrian refugees (whom he saw not as victims but as an Islamist national security threat). His statements also suggested that he would ride roughshod over human rights sensitivities when building his border wall.

For Mexico, then, a Trump presidency threatened to make life unpleasant. For already precarious regions like the Korean peninsula or the Persian Gulf, it might render them even less safe. Cumulatively, all this was likely to cause considerable disruption and had the potential to unravel many of the webs of international society carefully woven over the past 60 years or so. Trump had repeatedly declared, over a number of years, that he did not believe the United States should be the global policeman. While the US would step up the number of global drone strikes and bombing raids in the War on Terror, he acknowledged during the campaign that it would cease to exercise a general superintendence over the defence of democracy and human rights.[11] However, that did not mean that Trump as president would refrain from justifying potential interventions in humanitarian language. Media coverage of humanitarian atrocities can lead to public outrage and encourage a president to intervene, as occurred with George H.W. Bush in Somalia and Bill Clinton in the

Balkans. Trump, a notoriously avid watcher of cable news, had shown in the past his susceptibility to the so-called "CNN effect" (even if he now lambasts the network itself as "fake news.")[12] Indeed, as we have seen, he was initially a supporter of the US intervention in Libya, justifying it, in part, on humanitarian grounds. Trump was adamant, however, that Libya "should pay us back" by reimbursing the United States with oil.[13] A consistent refrain when commenting on overseas US interventions was that any action should materially benefit the United States, either through resource acquisition or financial recompense reflecting his favourite dictum – "to the victor the spoils". This did not preclude the prospect of Trump-led interventions, then, but suggested those undertaken would be more nakedly transactional and acquisitive than humanitarian in nature.

Trump's rhetoric pointed towards an initial "pivot" of US foreign policy towards the Middle East and the Mediterranean. In Syria, the new administration outlined its intention to seek cooperation with Russia and the Assad regime against ISIS, if necessary in return for concessions elsewhere. In this respect, the ways in which Trump and Putin conceived of their nation's core interests were complementary. While Putin saw Russia's engagement in Syria as a way of distracting attention from its campaign in Ukraine, Trump made clear that he regarded American concern for Ukraine as a diversion from its principal security threat, Islamist terrorism. Trump's attitude suggested that he might turn a blind eye to Russian actions in Eastern Europe in exchange for cooperation on the destruction of

ISIS. That appeared to only be the start, however. Trump's hostility to the nuclear deal with Iran and the regime was a matter of record, and the writings of Mike Flynn – his first pick for NSA – had been only slightly less anti-Iranian than they had been anti-ISIS. In Trump's campaign rhetoric, dealing with Raqqa might come first, but Tehran was next. How exactly it intended to go about this was not obvious, but the planned new 350-ship navy was clearly not needed to deal just with ISIS.

Secondly, President Trump repeatedly declared he would take on China, at least with regard to trade, not least because it was critical to his domestic jobs programme. He promised to designate China as a currency manipulator and also impose whopping tariffs on Chinese goods. In this connection, it seemed significant that President Trump had expressed enthusiasm for Stefan Halper's book *The Beijing Consensus*[14], which takes an understandably dim view of China's restrictive trade practices, authoritarian proclivities and regional belligerence. Even more suggestive was the appointment of the economist and academic Peter Navarro, a longstanding critic of China's trade policies, to head up the new National Trade Council.

Initially, Chinese leaders seemed to be contemplating the prospect of a Trump Presidency with remarkable insouciance. They appeared to regard him as one of their own, a man who would not bother them with human rights sermons, and with whom they could do business.[15] However, it increasingly became clear to them that this was the problem. Trump shared their zero-sum view of the world, and explicitly intended to prevail at their expense. As that realisation began to dawn, Chinese officials evinced increasing concern about the consequences of a trade war.[16] That said, economics aside, there was little sign yet that President Trump had a broader political, ideological or military agenda with respect to China. His remarks, both recent and longstanding, suggested that he had little interest in maintaining alliances with South Korea, Japan and other states keen to contain Beijing unless they paid vastly more to support the maintenance of US forces in the region, costs that those nations indicated they were unprepared to bear. When combined with Trump's resolve to pull out of the Trans-Pacific Partnership, which his predecessor had spent his entire term urging US allies to join, and his lumping of Japan and South Korea with China as nations that economically exploited the United States, America's traditional friends had little reason to count on its continued commitment to their security and prosperity.

As for Syria, Trump's campaign rhetoric did not appear to take into account that the bulk of Syrian government forces and the vast majority of Russian air strikes were directed against the rebels, not ISIS. Those fighting ISIS were the Kurds, the Western powers and (admittedly not very effectively) the rebels. In the aftermath of his election, however, Trump reiterated his contempt for the Syrian rebels and indicated that an Assad victory was preferable so that he could concentrate all his fire on ISIS.

In Israel, Trump's victory was greeted by some Israeli right-wingers as an endorsement for future intransigence. Naftali Bennett, the leader of the hard-line nationalist Jewish Home party, declared that, as a result of Trump's victory, the "era of the Palestinian state is over" as this was "the President-Elect's outlook as it appears in his platform."[17] It is true that the new President had trumpeted his commitment to Israel, referencing his various donations to, and involvement with, Israel related causes. He had taken a hawkish stance on Israel during the campaign and stated his intention to move the US Embassy to Jerusalem as soon as he took office. And after winning the election, he appointed a staunch supporter of West Bank settlements, David Friedman, as his ambassador to Israel.

But a closer look revealed a different picture. Trump had consistently stated his ambition to secure peace between Israel and the Palestinians. Back in 2007 in an interview with the British weekly the *Observer*, Trump suggested that if he became president "first, I'd try and solve the problems in the Middle East – that could be solved … Everything can be solved if you have talent."[18] During the 2016 Republican primaries, Trump declared his intention to be "neutral" on the Israeli–Palestinian conflict, to give himself the best chance of making "the toughest deal in the world." In a *Wall Street Journal* interview on 11 November, two days after his election victory, he referred to peace between Israel and the Palestinians as the "ultimate deal" and declared that, "as a dealmaker, I'd like to do … the deal that can't be made."[19] Yet, as previous presidents have discovered, the Israeli–Palestinian conflict does not occur in a vacuum and is extremely sensitive to shifts in the wider region. In particular, the relative calm between Israel and its neighbors could be shattered at any time by Hamas and Hezbollah, who have both amassed substantial arsenals of long-range rockets through their principal supplier, Iran. How Trump plans to confront Iran without imperiling his ambition to achieve Israeli–Palestinian peace remains to be seen.

In East Asia, there was a danger that a trade war might not only precipitate another world recession, but also a full-scale military confrontation. China took its time responding to President Trump's election, and when it did so it was with extreme truculence. Beijing vowed to retaliate against any tariffs. Although their initial public response to Trump's post-election telephone conversation with the president of Taiwan appeared relatively mild, reports suggested that China's leaders were furious about Trump's open rhetorical breach of the "One China" policy.[20] In the lead up to the Trump inauguration, China sent its sole aircraft carrier into the Taiwan Strait in a clear show of force. If backed into a corner, Beijing indicated that it might well try "horizontal escalation" in places like Taiwan or the South China Sea. For example, it might respond with military moves against the imposition of harsh tariffs. Unless the new president was entirely clear about how he would react, and this required him either to reaffirm the existing strategic architecture of the region or to signal his disengagement from East Asia, then the chances of a catastrophic misunderstanding were high.

By far the greatest risk to the international system, however, was not a war that President Trump might start, but the one that he had already signalled that he might not fight, and would thus fail to deter. His rallies often featured banners accusing Hillary Clinton of wanting to start "World War III." These referred to her willingness to honour US commitments under the collective defence provisions of Article 5 of the NATO charter. Trump, by contrast, had repeatedly questioned whether the US should defend allies who were not spending enough on their own protection. He even referred to NATO as "obsolete." More worryingly, there was a general whiff of pro-Russianism in the Trump camp. The President-elect had made no secret of his personal admiration for Vladimir Putin, the man who annexed Crimea, unleashed a proxy war in eastern Ukraine and threatened NATO's eastern flank, to say nothing of his other crimes. This seemed to reflect not only a sense of Trump's priorities and *realpolitik*, but an active preference for the Russian leader and his style of politics.

A striking thing about Trump's otherwise obscure foreign policy team during the presidential election campaign was its closeness to Moscow. One of his most trusted former confidants, Paul Manafort, had served as a long-term public relations advisor to the disgraced former President of Ukraine and Russian stooge, Viktor Yanukovich. Another advisor, Carter Page, was likewise an apologist for the Russian regime. One of Trump's main backers, Newt Gingrich, had even described Estonia as a mere "suburb" of St Petersburg.[21] The close Russian connections of many others in President Trump's penumbra were too numerous and too well known to require repetition here. The frightening truth was that with regard to Russia there was a lot more going on in the Trump camp than just – entirely understandable – irritation with European free-riding. Many Americans were angry that the United States was forced to shoulder 72 per cent of NATO's annual budget and tired of underwriting what critics have termed a "military welfare state."[22] Robert Gates, Defense Secretary under both George W. Bush and Barack Obama had cautioned Europeans that their refusal to invest sufficient funds in their own defence risked dooming the alliance to a "dim and dismal future."[23] But, before Trump, no major American policymaker had so vehemently and publicly questioned the relevance of NATO and thrown doubt on the US commitment to upholding its charter.

All this reflected a much broader, and deeply troubling, "de-Europeanisation" of the American strategic mind, if not necessarily in national security circles then in politics and among the population at large. Once upon a time, a strong stance against the Soviet Union united both Cold War liberals and the working class, particularly amongst the significant number whose families originally hailed from Poland, Ukraine and the Baltic. Gerald Ford's gaffe in a televised 1976 election debate, in which he denied that Eastern Europe was then under Soviet dominance, may have cost him the White House. Likewise, many of the "Reagan Democrats" of the 1980s – primarily disaffected blue collar workers, a number with Eastern European immigrant backgrounds – wanted the US to stand up to the Kremlin. That constituency is no more and it is a sign of the times that Gingrich, who had written support for the integration of former Warsaw Pact countries into NATO into his "Contract for America" 20 years ago, should now hold the alliance so cheap.[24] All the same, it was surprising to see the flippancy and vehemence with which a 60-year transatlantic bond had been put in question, not reluctantly but with a whooping yell.

Everything pointed to a President Trump lifting sanctions on Putin before time and recognising his annexation of the Crimea, legitimising the first forcible annexation of territory in Europe since World War II. A new "Yalta" seemed to beckon, in which the United States conceded a wide "sphere of influence" to Mr Putin in return for concessions and cooperation on the War on Terror. By throwing doubt on America's commitment to upholding the NATO charter, Trump had undermined the value of the alliance's Article 5 collective security guarantee, under which all signatories commit to the defence of fellow members if they are attacked. In doing so, he risked placing Poland, the Baltic and the Black Sea states in the firing line. Trump seemed oblivious to this danger, largely because his principal concerns were economic and he did not see Russia as a serious competitor with the US in this realm. It was surprising, given his general belligerence, that Trump's rhetoric did not appear to take other factors, such as ideology or raw military power much into account.

Geopolitically, the results of all this were entirely uncertain but threatened to lead to a completely different global strategic balance. Europe was at risk of finding itself, effectively, on its own against Russia and in the defence of Western values worldwide. President Putin might be emboldened to take risks, in Ukraine, in Eastern and Northern Europe, and more generally. On the other hand, he might prefer to explore a strategic partnership with President Trump.

Of course, the past three presidents had also sought to improve US–Russian relations, with little long term success. However, Trump had expressed greater sympathy for the Kremlin's critique of the post-Cold World order than his predecessors. Previous attempts to improve relations between the two countries mainly foundered on tensions in Europe. The US had supported both NATO and the EU as pillars on which European order rests, but Russia had railed against those institutions for excluding it from the continent's governance. Russian aggression against its neighbours had antagonised Washington.[25] However, Trump's dismissal of the European Union as "basically a vehicle for Germany," and his disdain for NATO as "obsolete," partly on the basis that "it was designed many, many years ago," coupled with his refusal to commit to upholding the organisation's Article 5 guarantee, encouraged the Kremlin's belief that the European order could soon be reconfigured in its favour.[26] Indeed, Trump's open hostility to the European Union – the principal instrument of European continental order long supported by US policymakers – added yet another problem to the long list already confronting Brussels and the national governments. As if this were not bad enough, Trump's election victory also encouraged the European "deplorables": the Alternative für Deutschland in Germany, Orbán's Hungary and the French National Front. All this meant that the capacity of the European Union to deal with its myriad security, economic and migration challenges was likely to be severely tested.

To put it in language that Trump knows best, that of real estate, the problem is not so much his belief that diplomacy is "transactional" – all political relationships are – but that he takes a very short-term and narrow view, privileging the quick buck over long-term shareholder value. It is perfectly true that many of the European tenants are not paying their contribution to the common defence, but some are. The problem with Trump's approach is that he has no satisfactory way of specifically punishing the transgressors. If he were to turn off the heating, everyone would freeze. Besides, some of the worst offenders, in the Mediterranean, live in south facing apartments away from the cold Russian wind. They would be the last to feel the drop in temperature.

The people most affected by Trump's stance on Article 5, especially the Baltic States, are guilty of nothing more than being born in the best property in a terrible part of town. If he withdraws NATO insurance cover, property prices would go down and people would move out. This is because collective security works rather like Bill Bratton's New York. It depends on zero tolerance, on fixing the windows and apprehending the stone throwers. The danger was that after four years of Trump, much of Eastern Europe could resemble a declining neighbourhood in 1980s America, with broken windows, uncollected rubbish, and demoralised residents huddled around braziers trying not to catch the eye of the criminals stalking their streets.

Nevertheless, in the aftermath of his election, Europe's leaders continued to misread Trump's world view and misunderstand the depth of his convictions. After Trump dismissed NATO as "obsolete" and threatened to impose punitive import taxes on foreign car makers, the German foreign minister, Frank-Walter Steinmeier, then in Brussels for a conference with his counterparts from other EU countries, said that these remarks had caused "astonishment and agitation" among his colleagues.[27] And yet not only had Trump stated these things repeatedly during the 2016 campaign, but he had also been saying them in numerous interviews over the past three decades, as this book has shown. As he had informed *Playboy* in 1990, if he ever became president then his first act would be to "throw a tax on every Mercedes-Benz rolling into this country."[28] And as he told Larry King in 1987, he believed NATO was "taking tremendous advantage" of the United States and that America's allies should "make a major contribution to this country" to ensure their continued protection.[29]

A number of politicians and foreign policy analysts suggested that, while Trump might have held these views for a long time, he would surely temper or abandon those views once he was in office and faced with global realities. However, as the Brookings Institution scholar Thomas Wright astutely noted, "at 70 years old, having held these beliefs for the better part of 30 years, he's unlikely at the moment of complete vindication in his own mind to change his policy when he hasn't so far."[30]

It is true that cataclysmic world events forced past presidents to shift their positions. For example, George W. Bush and his administration entered office in 2001 expressing opposition to the nation building that had characterised the Bill Clinton presidency and stressing their intention to avoid sending American troops to participate in regional conflicts. But the unprecedented terrorist attacks on 11 September 2001 fundamentally altered the administration's foreign policy priorities. It could be that unforeseen events might occur over the next four years that would compel President Trump to abandon his longest held positions. Nevertheless, what was clear was that when Donald Trump entered the White House, he did so with a world view that had been constantly advanced and relatively consistently articulated in countless statements over the past three decades. Don't say he didn't warn you.

EPILOGUE

PRESIDENT TRUMP VS THE WORLD: THE FIRST 100 DAYS

"I really don't change my position very much." This is how President Donald Trump responded to the charge, levelled during a press conference at the end of his first week in office, that his foreign policy statements were inconsistent. The new President told journalists to "go back and look, my position on trade has been solid for many, many years, since I was a very young person talking about how we were getting ripped off by the rest of the world."[1] As this book has shown, Trump had been remarkably consistent in his comments about US trade relations for three decades. Trump could also have added that his position on the North Atlantic Treaty Organization (NATO) and the USA's East Asian alliances had not changed much prior to assuming the presidency. He had consistently argued that the USA was "getting ripped off" by its allies, claiming that they provided insufficient compensation for the protection that they received and then took advantage of it on trade. His longstanding skepticism that the USA should attempt to spread its liberal and democratic values around the world was well documented, as was his affinity for "tough" leaders, even if they presided over autocratic or authoritarian regimes. His attitude to overseas US interventions had also been relatively "solid," with Trump invariably suggesting that engagements must result in a financial gain or the obtainment of resources. He had repeatedly attacked previous US presidents for their incompetence and argued that it would only require one forceful leader to ensure that the USA achieved definite and decisive international triumphs again. Before assuming office, Trump had developed a consistently expressed, if roughly defined, set of positions on these issues, which, taken together, comprised the rudiments of his world view. Yet, as Trump himself admitted during his press conference, "now, I never knew I'd be in the position where we can actually do something about it."[2]

At the time of writing, Trump has had 100 days in the White House. The "First 100 days" has been a yardstick of presidential success since Franklin Roosevelt's first few months in office, during which he vigorously tackled the Great Depression through a blitz of legislation and by relaying a message of relentless optimism to a disillusioned and economically distressed nation. As Trump passes that landmark it is an appropriate juncture to assess whether his world view is still discernible and, if so, how it has fared when faced with the realities of high office.

President Trump entered office with an inaugural address that clearly reflected the nationalist strategy that he had championed during his campaign and for three decades previously. His "position on trade" was evident in his commitment to "protect our borders from the ravages of other countries making our products, stealing our companies, and destroying our jobs: Protection will lead to great prosperity and strength." The desire for definitive victories was summed up in his declaration, "America will start winning again, winning like never before" and his promise that "Radical Islamic Terrorism" would be "eradicate[d] completely from the face of the Earth." He railed against previous administrations, who he claimed "enriched foreign industry at the expense of American industry, subsidised the armies of other countries while allowing for the very sad depletion of our military" and "defended other nation's borders while refusing to defend our own." And he stated categorically that "from this moment on, it's going to be America First."[3]

He quickly looked to turn those words into actions. Much of what the President enacted over the following weeks was entirely predictable on the basis of his pre-presidential rhetoric. Within days of entering office, Trump had withdrawn from the Trans-Pacific Partnership, keeping a promise that he had reiterated throughout his campaign. The following week the administration announced that it would be imposing sanctions on Iran for its recent missile test. In characteristic fashion, President Trump reinforced this announcement with a tweet, saying: "Iran is playing with fire – they don't appreciate how 'kind' President

Obama was to them. Not me!"[4] This reflected Trump's campaign rhetoric that the Obama administration was insufficiently tough on Iran, but also his deep animus toward the regime in Tehran which, as we had noted, had been evident in his public statements since the hostage crisis of 1980. And he doubled down, at least initially, on his campaign pledge to fortify the border wall with Mexico.

While Trump has made some boilerplate statements on NATO's historic achievements and rubber-stamped the Senate's vote on admitting Montenegro, there has also been sufficient evidence that he retains his belief that America's allies should be paying more in compensation for the protection that it provides and that he remains unconvinced about the alliance's core mission. After meeting with the German Chancellor Angela Merkel in Washington, DC, Trump tweeted that "Germany owes vast sums of money to NATO and the US must be paid more for the powerful, and very expensive, defense, it provides to Germany."[5] On top of this, it was widely reported that Trump handed Merkel a bill for $374 billion, reflecting the amount by which Germany has supposedly fallen short in its targeted defence spending since 2002.[6] Rather than simply a statement that European allies should be meeting the 2 per cent of GDP they committed to spend on defence, this was a conspicuous illustration of Trump's continued transactional attitude to the USA's alliances, which he had expressed in foreign policy statements stretching back to the late 1980s. Furthermore, although Trump suggested that he no longer believed NATO was "obsolete," as he had argued during the presidential campaign, this was based on his assertion that he had forced the alliance to do more to fight terrorism. Leaving aside the fact that NATO had already deployed troops to Afghanistan for more than a decade as part of the War on Terror, Trump has not yet explicitly stated his support for NATO's crucial Article 5 clause, that an "armed attack against one" Nato member "shall be considered an attack against them all". During the campaign, Trump had stated that he would predicate his commitment to honoring NATO's collective security guarantee on whether a country had paid its "fair share," stating that the US needed to "get money" from its allies and suggesting that "we're gonna end up in World War Three protecting people and these people can pay."[7] After 100 days in office it still remains unclear whether Trump believes that Article 5 constitutes a binding obligation on the US to aid any NATO ally that is the victim of external aggression.

We had previously suggested that the USA, under Trump, would not exercise a general superintendence over the defence of democracy and human rights. This quickly became clear as Trump expressed little concern and immediately congratulated the Turkish President Recep Tayyip Erdoğan for winning his referendum despite widespread charges of fraud during the campaign and the authoritarian crackdown that has followed in its wake. Of course, most American leaders have prioritised strategic interests over democratic ideals when allying with authoritarian leaders, a realist position best encapsulated by Franklin Roosevelt's alleged comment about one Latin American dictator:

"He's a son of a bitch, but he's our son of a bitch."[8] But few US presidents have been so willing to publicly signal that the nation's values would play little role in the conduct of their administration's foreign policy. Early in his presidency, Trump responded to the talk show host Bill O'Reilly's statement that Russian President Vladimir Putin was a "killer" by stating that the USA "have a lot of killers" and was not so "innocent" itself.[9] Trump's remarks not only echoed a similar assertion made during the campaign but continued a longstanding theme in his rhetoric that the US had no right to lecture other nations on human rights because it was no more exceptional or virtuous than other countries.

Yet, as we previously noted, this did not preclude President Trump from engaging in military interventions in response to harrowing televised images of atrocities and couching his actions in humanitarian rhetoric. Trump's sanctioning of cruise missile strikes against President Bashar al-Assad's regime in Syria may have been a reversal of his earlier, repeated statements that President Obama should avoid bombing the country in response to the use of chemical weapons and his campaign pledges to work with Russia to back the Syrian leader against ISIS. But, as we suggested, it was in keeping with his susceptibility to the "CNN effect," illustrated in his initial response to the 2011 Libyan rebellion, and reflected his stated preference for the remote use of air power in interventions. The missile strikes were accompanied by an impassioned appeal that "no child of God should ever suffer such horror."[10] The Syrian action also deflected attention from two domestic defeats, by the courts over his travel ban and by Congress over healthcare, and allowed him to nakedly laud the strike as a "win." In addition, it allowed him to present himself as the polar opposite of his predecessor, blaming the chemical attack on Obama's "weakness and irresolution" in drawing a red line and then refusing to act on it, even while acting without the congressional approval that he had previously declared was necessary if Obama acted in Syria.[11]

We had made little mention earlier of Trump's potential policies with respect to North Korea, but his decision to dispatch an aircraft carrier to the waters off the Korean peninsula reflected the same desire to garner "respect" from rogue regimes and tin-pot dictators that he had first exhibited in his response to the Iranian hostage crisis, 37 years previously.

Dealing with the threat posed by North Korea has also led Trump to walk back his pledges to label China as a currency manipulator and to slap large punitive tariffs on Chinese imports to the US. At present, he is seeking to entice Beijing into co-operating on addressing Pyongynag's provocations, but he has also declared that the US will act unilaterally on the nuclear issue if necessary. Despite his tough rhetoric, Trump's wider strategy in the region remains a prisoner to his transactional view of US alliances. Even while confronting Pyongyang, he threatened to terminate a free trade agreement with South Korea, that he described as "horrible," and demanded that Seoul pay for the $1 billion Terminal High Altitude Area Defense (THAAD) anti-ballistic missile system.[12] While Trump has touted his "unpredictability" in foreign policy as an asset, Trump's transactional approach to America's alliances in Europe and East Asia remains the most predictable aspect of his foreign policy.

Back in a 1990 *Playboy* interview, Trump had stated that, as president, he would "believe very strongly in military strength" and, in keeping with this, his proposed budget called for a $54 billion increase in defence spending.[13] He gave the military "total authorisation" to deploy the "mother of all bombs," the largest non-nuclear device ever used by the US, against Islamic State positions in Afghanistan. While Trump has come to closely identify with what he has referred to as "my military" and has given his generals substantial leeway in tactical operations, he has proposed a 29 per cent cut to the State Department's budget.[14] Instead, his emphasis on leadership has led him to focus on personal diplomacy and to talk up the "unbelievable chemistry" that he has developed with other global leaders, notably such "tough" figures as Egyptian President Abdel Fattah el-Sisi and Chinese Premier Xi Jinping.[15] While the investigations surrounding the Trump campaign's ties with Russia and the decision to strike the Syrian airbase has complicated his oft expressed desire to build a rapport with Vladimir Putin, the president has not given up on this ambition. As his head of strategic communications for the National Security Council, Michael Anton, recently stated, Trump was "still hopeful that the relationship can get better, and that he can even build a positive relationship with Vladimir Putin."[16]

Throughout the first 100 days, analysts have speculated as to how the standing of various advisors offer insights into the direction of the administration's foreign policy. The elevation of Steve Bannon, Trump's Chief Strategist, to the National Security Council was seen as evidence that a nationalist stance would dictate US foreign policy, while his removal two months later was taken as a sign that internationalism was back in fashion. The forced resignation of Michael Flynn as National Security Advisor (after news broke of contacts with Russian officials during the campaign and prior to the inauguration despite Flynn's assurances to Vice President Mike Pence to the contrary) and his ultimate replacement by General H.R. McMaster, were taken as an indication that "grown-ups" would now be running US foreign policy. McMaster has certainly professionalised the National Security process and, together with Secretary of Defence James Mattis and Secretary of State Rex Tillerson, constitutes a cadre of advisers committed to NATO and US leadership of the liberal international order more broadly. McMaster has spoken cogently on the need to ensure that the US begins to "think in competitive terms again." Widespread respect for McMaster, coupled with his decision to appoint Nadia Schadlow, who has shrewdly written on how the US must predicate its policies on the "serious political competitions underway for regional and strategic domination," led commentators to hope that this might lead to a more sophisticated version of Trump's campaign slogan, "we need to start winning again."[17]

We hope that this is the case. But, whatever tactical shifts these advisers are able to execute, we remain skeptical that this will lead to a broader "normalisation" of Trump's foreign policy and grand strategy. Firstly, as we made clear earlier and as these 100 days have illustrated, Trump can drop advisers as quickly as he elevates them and there is no guarantee that those figures most committed to continued US leadership of the post-1945 world order, and most perceptive of the need to make it strategically competitive, will triumph in the bureaucratic competition. Secondly, the emerging structure of Trump's foreign policy, according to the *Washington Post*'s Josh Rogin, depends on a "top-down approach" and is based on US officials turning Trump's "America First" campaign pledges into policies. Administration officials are expected to base their positions on "what Trump has said on issues" in the past.[18] This was particularly evident, just after the 100 days mark, in Tillerson's address to his staff outlining how Trump's "America First" agenda translates into a foreign policy.

The Secretary drew a clear distinction between American values and its policies, and baldly suggested that the administration would de-emphasise human rights concerns when it created "obstacles to our ability to advance our national security interests, our economic interests."[19]

Finally, the man who most matters in shaping US foreign policy remains the president himself. As we suggested previously, the relatively untrammeled power that the president has to shape the nation's foreign policy would make this axiomatic in almost any administration. But it is particularly the case with Trump who, when questions were swirling about the influence of various factions in the White House, again made it clear that he was the man setting policy: "I'm my own strategist."[20] As a consequence, the need to understand the formation of Trump's worldview and the core convictions that he brought to the White House remains as urgent as ever.

NOTES

INTRODUCTION

1. Paul Kennedy, *The Rise and Fall of the Great Powers* (New York, 1987), pp. 357–9.
2. Denis William Brogan, "The illusion of American omnipotence", *Harper's Magazine*, December 1952.
3. Trump advertisement in the *Washington Post*, *New York Times* and *Boston Globe*, 2 September 1987.
4. Interview with Larry King, CNN, 2 September 1987.
5. Donald Trump, Presidential campaign announcement speech,' 16 June 2015.
6. Interview with Glenn Plaskin, *Playboy*, March 1990.
7. Trump, Announcement Speech, 16 June 2015.
8. Donald Trump, Speech to Republican women's groups in Las Vegas, Nevada, 29 April 2011.
9. Trump, Announcement Speech, 16 June 2015.
10. Interview with George Stephanopoulos, ABC News, 18 April 2011.
11. Trump, Announcement Speech, 16 June 2015.
12. Interview with Rona Barrett (NBC, "Rona Barrett Looks at Today's Super Rich"), 6 October 1980.

13. Ibid.
14. Trump advertisement in the *Washington Post*, *New York Times* and *Boston Globe*, 2 September 1987.
15. Interview with Glenn Plaskin, *Playboy*, March 1990.
16. Trump, Announcement Speech, 16 June 2015.
17. Donald Trump, Republican Nomination Acceptance Speech, 21 July 2016.
18. Salena Zito, "Taking Trump seriously, not literally," *The Atlantic*, 23 September 2016.

CHAPTER 1: IMPERIAL OVERSTRETCH: THE INTELLECTUAL ROOTS OF TRUMPISM ABROAD

1. On numerous occasions, Trump himself invoked and celebrated the seventh president of the United States during his 2016 presidential campaign, and hung a portrait of him in the Oval Office, although he and his aides have focused on Jackson's populist challenge to the political establishment more than explicit references to his foreign policy ideas. For more on the Jacksonian tradition in American foreign policy see Walter Russell Mead, *Special Providence: American Foreign Policy and How it Changed the World* (New York, 2001) and "The Jacksonian Revolt," *Foreign Affairs*, January 20th 2017.
2. Trump, Acceptance Speech, 21 July 2016.
3. For more on the use of the "America First" slogan in Wilson's 1916 presidential campaign see Steven A. Seidman, *Posters, Propaganda, and Persuasion in Election Campaigns Around the World and Through History* (New York, 2008), p. 54.
4. Warren G. Harding, (edited by Fredrick E. Schortemeier) *Rededicating America: Life and Recent Speeches of Warren G. Harding* (Indianapolis, 1920), p. 81.

5. The most in-depth and detailed analysis of the "America First Committee" is Justus D. Doenecke (ed.), *In Danger Undaunted: The Anti-Interventionist Movement of 1940–1941 as Revealed in the Papers of the America First Committee* (Stanford, CA, 1990).

6. For more on Buchanan's "America First" campaign see Derek Chollet and James Goldgeier, *America Between the Wars: From 11/9 to 9/11: The Misunderstood Years Between the Fall of the Berlin Wall and Start of the War on Terror* (New York, 2008), pp. 23–35.

7. For Trump's comments see Interview with Larry King, CNN, 8 October 1999. For Buchanan's original remarks see Patrick Buchanan, *A Republic Not an Empire: Reclaiming America's Destiny* (Washington DC, 1999).

8. Trump advertisement in the *Washington Post, New York Times* and *Boston Globe*, 2 September 1987.

9. John A. Thompson, *A Sense of Power: The Roots of America's Global Role* (Ithaca, NY: Cornell University Press, 2015), pp. 27–36.

10. Ibid, p. 30.

11. John A. Thompson, "The appeal of 'America First' in Donald Trump's America," *E-International Relations*, 15 January 2017.

CHAPTER 2: NOVICE: WEALTH AND THE NATION, 1980–2000

1. Polly Toynbee, "Towering Trump – The tycoon is big on himself and it has paid handsomely, but what can he do for the people?", *Guardian*, 26 May 1988.

2. *Washington Post* interview with Rona Barrett by Robert Samuels' in "'Trump Revealed': The reporting archive," 30 August 2016. Available at https://www.washingtonpost.com/graphics/politics/trump-revealed-book-reporting-archive/.

3. Trump advertisement in the *Washington Post, New York Times* and *Boston Globe*, 2 September 1987.

4. Examples include David Halberstam, "Can we rise to the Japanese challenge? *Parade*, 9 October 1983; Ezra Vogel, "Pax Nipponica?" *Foreign Affairs* 64/4 (Spring 1986); T.H. White, "The danger from Japan," *New York Times Magazine*, 28 July 1985. For more on the widespread American concern about the growth of Japan in this period see Jennifer Miller, "Adam Smith's arthiritis: Japan and the fear of American decline," Paper delivered at conference: Ronald Reagan and the Transformation of Global Politics in the 1980s, Austin, Texas, 20 January 2017. (Paper in possession of author.)

5. Paul Kennedy, *The Rise and Fall of the Great Powers: Economic Change and Military Conflict from 1500 to 2000* (Random House: New York, 1987), pp. 514–15.

6. Ibid, pp. 416–18.

7. For Trump's comments see "Appearance on the *Phil Donahue Show*," WNBC, 16 December 1987.

8. Kennedy, *The Rise and Fall of the Great Powers*, pp. 416–18, 439.

9. David S. Cloud, "How much do allies pay for U.S. troops? A lot more than Donald Trumps says," *Los Angeles Times*, 1 October 2016.

10. Edward A. Olsen, *U.S.–Japan Strategic Reciprocity: A Neo-Internationalist View* (Stanford, CA: Hoover Institution Press, 1985), p. 92.

11. https://www.washingtonpost.com/wp-stat/graphics/politics/trump-archive/docs/rona-barrett-1980-interview-of-donald-trump.pdf.

12. Toynbee, "Towering Trump," *Guardian*, 26 May 1988. For Trump's fondness for *The Godfather* see Tom Brook, "Presidential contenders make cautious movie picks," *BBC Magazine*, 7 April 2016.

13. Steve Eder and Dave Phillips, "Donald Trump's draft deferments: Four for college, one for bad feet," *New York Times*, 1 August 2016.

14. David Reynolds, *One World Divisible: A Global History Since 1945* (New York: W.W. Norton & Company, 2000), pp. 382–4.

15. https://www.washingtonpost.com/archive/lifestyle/1984/11/15/donald-trump-holding-all-the-cards-the-tower-the-team-the-money-the-future/8be79254-7793-4812-a153-f2b88e81fa54/?utm_term=.42e62394c2a5.

16. Quoted in Gil Troy, *The Reagan Revolution: A Very Short Introduction* (New York: Oxford University Press, 2009), p. 37.

17. Michael Kruse, "He brutalized for you," *Politico*, 8 April 2016. Available at http://www.politico.com/magazine/story/2016/04/donald-trump-roy-cohn-mentor-joseph-mccarthy-213799.

18. Jonathan Broder, "Gulf allies hinder mine sweep,' *Chicago Tribune*, 29 July 1987; [LA] Times Wire Services," "Minesweeper copters to be sent to Gulf: Departure from U.S. 'imminent'; No oil convoy delay seen," *Los Angeles Times*, 29 July 1987.

19. http://edition.cnn.com/videos/tv/2016/05/09/donald-trump-1987-interview-larry-king-live.cnn.

20. http://www.nytimes.com/1987/10/23/nyregion/new-hampshire-speech-earns-praise-for-trump.html.

21. https://www.youtube.com/watch?v=ANrTNkfR_0I.

22. Quoted in Michael D'Antonio, *The Truth About Trump* (New York: Thomas Dunne Books, 2016), p. 185.

23. On Cohn's connections see Jonathan Mahler and Matt Flegenheimer, "What Donald Trump learned from Joseph McCarthy's right-hand man," *New York Times*, 20 June 2016. For Stone see Edward Luce, "Lunch with the FT: Roger Stone" *Financial Times*, 26 August 2016.

24. https://www.youtube.com/watch?v=GZpMJeynBeg.

25. https://www.youtube.com/watch?v=GmNN2MCJ-7U.

26. https://www.theguardian.com/commentisfree/2017/jan/12/polly-toynbee-1988-interview-donald-trump.

27. https://www.youtube.com/watch?v=NF3MwVvKOOQ.

28. https://www.youtube.com/watch?v=WojdgD8CB9g.

29. http://www.playboy.com/articles/playboy-interview-donald-trump-1990.

30. Lily Rothman, "When Trump tried to meet with a Soviet leader in the 1980s," *Time*, 18 October 2016. Available at http://time.com/4437403/trump-gorbachev-history/.

31. https://www.youtube.com/watch?v=ZXuTp7XF1nE.

32. http://www.miamiherald.com/news/local/community/miami-dade/article105154971.html.

33. Quoted in Patricia Mazzei, "Trump broke Cuban embargo, report says, roiling Miami politics," *Miami Herald*, 29 September 2016.

34. Kurt Eichenwald, "How Donald Trump's company violated the United States embargo against Cuba," *Newsweek*, 29 September 2016.

35. http://www.nytimes.com/1999/09/19/opinion/liberties-trump-l-oeil-tease.html.

36. Ben Hoyle, "Let Churchill inspire our alliance, May told Trump," *The Times*, 16 January 2017.
37. https://www.youtube.com/watch?v=peBa3SU46Qs.
38. See Patrick Buchanan, *A Republic Not an Empire: Reclaiming America's Destiny* (Washington DC, 1999).
39. Donald Trump (with Dave Shiflett), *The America We Deserve* (Los Angeles: Renaissance Books, 2000), p. 124.
40. Dave Shiflett, "Another time, another Trump," *Wall Street Journal*, 16 December 2015.
41. CNN.com, "Text of Clinton statement on Iraq, February 17 1998." Available at (http://edition.cnn.com/ALLPOLI-TICS/1998/02/17/transcripts/clinton.iraq/.

CHAPTER 3: APPRENTICE: PROTECTING THE NATION, 2001–14

1. Fareed Zakaria, "Excerpt: Zakaria's 'The post-American world,'" *Newsweek*, 3 May 2008.
2. http://www.politico.com/magazine/story/2016/09/trump-hillary-clinton-september-11-911-attacks-nyc-214236.
3. https://soundcloud.com/buzzfeedandrew/trump-on-the-howard-stern-show-on-sept-11-2002.
4. http://www.factcheck.org/2016/02/donald-trump-and-the-iraq-war/.
5. Ibid.
6. Ibid.
7. http://www.esquire.com/news-politics/a37230/donald-trump-esquire-cover-story-august-2004/.
8. http://edition.cnn.com/TRANSCRIPTS/0403/21/le.00.html.

9. http://www.playboy.com/articles/donald-trump-interview.

10. https://www.theguardian.com/business/2007/jan/07/media.citynews.

11. http://edition.cnn.com/TRANSCRIPTS/0904/15/lkl.01.html.

12. Extract from Donald Trump, with Meredith McIver, *Think Like a Champion: An Informal Education in Business and Life* (2009), p. 2.

13. https://www.youtube.com/watch?v=DNEC9shlLqk.

14. http://transcripts.cnn.com/TRANSCRIPTS/1012/08/joy.01.html.

15. https://www.c-span.org/video/?297952-12/donald-trump-remarks.

16. https://www.youtube.com/watch?v=OTqoz0RYvVM.

17. http://transcripts.cnn.com/TRANSCRIPTS/1103/28/pmt.01.html.

18. http://www.foxnews.com/transcript/2011/03/30/donaldtrump-sits-down-bill-oreilly/.

19. http://www.foxnews.com/transcript/2011/03/31/donald-trump-oreilly-factor-part-2/.

20. http://www.foxnews.com/transcript/2011/04/01/donald-trump-afghanistan-2012/.

21. http://blogs.abcnews.com/george/2011/04/donald-trump-interview-transcript-part-one.html.

22. http://latimesblogs.latimes.com/washington/2011/05/donald-trump-i-understand-the-chinese-mind.html.

23. https://asiancorrespondent.com/2011/06/china-expats-polarized-by-trumps-literary-cocktail/.

24. http://www.foxnews.com/transcript/2011/12/13/inside-story-trumps-gop-debate/.

25. http://transcripts.cnn.com/TRANSCRIPTS/1104/17/sotu.01.html.

26. http://edition.cnn.com/TRANSCRIPTS/1201/04/pmt.01.html.

27. http://edition.cnn.com/TRANSCRIPTS/1306/13/pmt.01.html.

28. http://edition.cnn.com/TRANSCRIPTS/1309/13/pmt.01.html.

29. http://edition.cnn.com/TRANSCRIPTS/1310/10/pmt.01.html.

30. http://www.msnbc.com/thomas-roberts/watch/watch-donald-trump-s-full-2013-interview-736112707862.

31. NBC News, "Trump and Putin tried to meet in Moscow three years ago: Source," *NBCnews.com*, 28 July 2016.Available at http://www.nbcnews.com/news/us-news/trump-putin-tried-meet-moscow-three-years-ago-source-n619006.

32. http://edition.cnn.com/TRANSCRIPTS/1312/11/pmt.01.html.

33. Donald Trump (with Tony Schwartz), *Trump: The Art of the Deal* (Ballantine Books: New York, 1987), p. 185.

34. https://www.c-span.org/video/?318134-9/donald-trump-addresses-cpac.

CHAPTER 4: CANDIDATE AND PRESIDENT-ELECT, 2015–17

1. Many academic "realists" have disputed Trump's claim to be one of them, however, and have distanced themselves from him. See Robert Kaplan, "On foreign policy, Donald Trump is no realist," *Washington Post*, 12 November 2016.

2. Donald J. Trump, Twitter post, 4:23pm and 4:30pm, December 4th 2016, http:/twitter.com/realdonaldtrump).

3. For quotes from Mattis see Rebecca Shabad, "James Mattis defends NATO, calls Russia a threat at confirmation hearing," *CBS News.com*, 12 January 2017. Available at http://www.cbsnews.com/news/james-mattis-defends-nato-calls-russia-a-threat-at-confirmation-hearing/. For a broader analysis of the clashing viewpoints in Trump's cabinet see Thomas Wright, "Order from chaos: Trump's team of rivals, riven by distrust," *Brookings.edu*, 15 December 2016. Available at https://www.brookings.edu/blog/order-from-chaos/2016/12/15/trumps-team-of-rivals-riven-by-distrust/.

4. Politico Staff, "Full transcript: Second 2016 presidential debate," *Politico.com*, 10 October 2016. Available at http://www.politico.com/story/2016/10/2016-presidential-debate-transcript-229519.

5. Lois Romano, "Donald Trump, holding all the cards: The tower! The team! The money! The future!" *Washington Post*, 15 November 1984.

6. Donald J. Trump (with Meredith McIver), *Think Like a Billionaire: Everything You Need to Know About Success, Real Estate, and Life* (Random House: New York, 2004), p. xxii.

7. Morning Joe, "Trump: My primary consultant is myself," *MSNBC.com*, 16 March 2016. Available at http://www.msnbc.com/morning-joe/watch/trump-my-primary-consultant-is-myself-645588035836.

8. Fox News Sunday, "Exclusive: Donald Trump on cabinet picks, transition process," *FoxNews.com*, 11 December 2016. Available at http://www.foxnews.com/transcript/2016/12/11/exclusive-donald-trump-on-cabinet-picks-transition-process/.

9. "Read Donald Trump's speech to Aipac," *Time.com*, 21 March 2016. Available at http://time.com/4267058/donald-trump-aipac-speech-transcript/.

10. John Bolton, *Surrender is Not an Option: Defending America at the United Nations and Abroad* (Threshold Editions: New York, 2008), p. 222.

11. Stephen Wertheim, "Trump and American exceptionalism", *Foreign Affairs*, 3 January 2017.

12. For more on "CNN Effect" see Theo Farrell, "Humanitarian intervention and peace operations," in John Baylis et al, (eds.) *Strategy in the Contemporary World* (Oxford: Oxford University Press, 2002) pp. 286–308.

13. "From the desk of Donald Trump," video posted by The Trump Organization, uploaded on 28 February 2011.

14. Stefan Halper, *The Beijing Consensus: Authoritarianism in Our Time* (New York: Basic Books, 2010).

15. Aaron Mak, "Why China's Not Afraid of Donald J. Trump," *Politico Magazine*, 8 May 2016.

16. This perspective was in evidence in the Chinese leader Xi Jinping's speech at the 2017 World Economic Forum. Charlie Campbell, "Xi Jinping Becomes an Unlikely Advocate of Free Trade at Davos," *Time*, January 17 2017, http://time.com/4635963/xi-jinping-china-davos-world-economic-forum-trade-donald-trump/.

17. Gil Hoffman, "Israeli right hails Trump: 'The era of a Palestinian state is over,' *Jpost.com*, 9 November 2016. Available at http://www.jpost.com/US-Elections/Donald-Trump/Likud-MKs-react-to-Trumps-victory-in-US-Presidential-Election-472088.

18. Gaby Wood, "Donald Trump: The interview," *Observer*, 7 January 2007.

19. Monica Langley and Gerard Baker, "Donald Trump, in exclusive interview, tells WSJ he is willing to keep parts of Obama's health law," *Wall Street Journal*, 11 November 2016.

20. "China media: Trump 'playing with fire' on Taiwan," *BBC.com*, 16 January 2017. Available at http://www.bbc.com/news/world-asia-china-38633257.

21. Reena Flores, "Newt Gingrich: NATO countries 'ought to worry' about U.S. commitment," *CBSnews.com*, 21 July 2016. Available at http://www.cbsnews.com/news/newt-gingrich-trump-would-reconsider-his-obligation-to-nato/.

22. Editorial, "NATO must rediscover its purpose, or it will end up losing a war," *Spectator*, 6 September 2014.

23. Thom Shanker, "Defense Secretary warns NATO of 'dim' future," *New York Times*, 10 June 2011.

24. James Kirchick, "How Trump got his party to love Russia," *Washingtonpost.com*, 6 January 2017. Available at https://www.washingtonpost.com/posteverything/wp/2017/01/06/how-trump-got-his-party-to-love-russia/?utm_term=.6c71601d089a.

25. For an excellent study that places future US–Russian relations in their historical context see Chris Miller, 'US–Russian Relations in the Next Presidency,' *German Marshall Fund*, Policy Brief, 7 December 2016.

26. For quotes see "Full Transcript of interview with Donald Trump," *The Times*, 16 January 2017.

27. Jacopo Barigazzi, "Germany's Steinmeier: NATO concerned at Trump Remarks," *Politico.eu*, 16 January 2017. Available at http://www.politico.eu/article/germany-foreign-minister-steinmeier-nato-concerned-at-us-president-donald-trump-remarks/.

28. Interview with Glenn Plaskin, *Playboy*, March 1990.

29. Interview with Larry King, CNN, 2 September 1987.

30. Uri Friedman, "How Donald Trump could change the world. An interview with Thomas Wright," *The Atlantic*, 7 September 2016.

EPILOGUE: PRESIDENT TRUMP VS THE WORLD: THE FIRST 100 DAYS

1. "Trump's Press Conference with British Prime Minister, Annotated," 27 January 2017, http://www.npr.org/2017/01/27/511985090/trumps-press-conference-with-british-prime-minister-annotated.

2. Ibid.

3. "The Inaugural Address," 20 January 2017, https://www.whitehouse.gov/inaugural-address.

4. Donald J. Trump, Twitter post, 3 February 2017, 3:28am, http:/twitter.com/realdonaldtrump.

5. Donald J. Trump, Twitter post, 18 March 2017, 6:23am. http:/twitter.com/realdonaldtrump.

6. Bojan Pancevski, 'Germany slams "intimidating" £300bn White House bill,' *Sunday Times*, 26 March 2017 https://www.thetimes.co.uk/article/germany-dismisses-white-houses-intimidating-300bn-bill-for-defence-dl7dk629k.

7. Ben Jacobs, 'Donald Trump reiterates he will only help NATO countries that pay "fair share," *Guardian*, 27 July 2016, https://www.theguardian.com/us-news/2016/jul/27/donald-trump-nato-isolationist.

8. Quoted in Robert Kagan, *A Twilight Struggle: American Power and Nicaragua, 1977–1990* (The Free Press: New York, 1996) p. 395.

9. "Preview: Trump Tells O'Reilly He 'Respects' Putin in Super Bowl Interview,' 4 February 2017, *Fox News insider*, http://insider.foxnews.com/2017/02/04/preview-bill-oreilly-donald-trump-super-bowl-interview.

10. "Full Transcript: Donald Trump Speech on Bashar Al-Assad and Ordering Strikes on Syria," *Newsweek*, http://www.newsweek.com/transcript-donald-trump-speech-order-syria-strikes-assad-580339.

11. Abby Phillip, "Trump blames Obama's 'weakness' for Assad's use of chemical weapons,' 4 April 2017, *Washington Post*, https://www.washingtonpost.com/news/post-politics/wp/2017/04/04/trump-blames-obamas-weakness-for-assads-use-of-chemical-weapons/?utm_term=.63d1372d4c85.

12. "Exclusive: Trump vows to fix or scrap South Korea trade deal, wants missile system payment," 28 April 2017, *Reuters* http://www.reuters.com/article/us-usa-trump-south-korea-exclusive-idUSKBN17U09M.

13. Interview with Glenn Plaskin, *Playboy,* March 1990.

14. "Trump: US military has been given total authorization," 13 April 2017, *Fox News*, http://video.foxnews.com/v/5397648241001/#sp=show-clips.

15. "Transcript of AP interview with Trump," 23 April 2017, *Washington Post*, https://www.washingtonpost.com/national/health-science/transcript-of-ap-interview-with-trump/2017/04/23/7c269138-284b-11e7-9081-f5405f56d3e4_story.html?utm_term=.a70913a16967.

16. Susan B. Glasser, "Michael Anton: The Full Transcript," 17 April 2017, *The Global Politico*, http://www.politico.com/magazine/story/2017/04/michael-anton-the-full-transcript-215029.

17. First quote in Gabriel Elefteriu, "General McMaster knows where the West went wrong, and can help President Trump make it right," 23 February 2017, *Daily Telegraph*, http://www.telegraph.co.uk/news/2017/02/23/general-mcmaster-knows-west-went-wrong-can-help-president-trump/; Second quote in Nadia Schadlow, "Welcome to the Competition," 26 January 2017, *War on the Rocks*, https://warontherocks.com/2017/01/welcome-to-the-competition/.

18. Josh Rogin, "There's no Trump foreign policy doctrine, but there is a structure," 27 April 2017, *Washington Post*, https://www.washingtonpost.com/news/josh-rogin/wp/2017/04/27/theres-no-trump-foreign-policy-doctrine-but-there-is-a-structure/?utm_term=.9def48b87792.

19. Rex Tillerson, 'Remarks to U.S. Department of State Employees,' 3 May 2017, https://www.state.gov/secretary/remarks/2017/05/270620.htm.

20. Michael Goodwin, 'Trump won't definitely say he still backs Bannon,' 11 April 2017, *New York Post*, http://nypost.com/2017/04/11/trump-wont-definitively-say-he-still-backs-bannon/.

BIBLIOGRAPHY

PRIMARY SOURCES

Books

Beahm, George, *Trump on Trump: Understanding Donald Trump through his own words* (Cassell Illustrated: London, 2016).

Trump, Donald (with Tony Schwartz), *Trump: The Art of the Deal* (Ballantine Books: New York, 1987).

Trump, Donald (with Kate Bohner), *The Art of the Comeback* (Times Books: New York, 1997).

Trump, Donald (with Dave Shiflett), *The America We Deserve* (Los Angeles: Renaissance Books, 2000).

Trump, Donald (with Meredith McIver), *Think Like a Billionaire: Everything You Need to Know About Success, Real Estate, and Life* (New York: Random House, 2004).

Trump, Donald (with Meredith McIver), *Think Like a Champion: An Informal Education in Business and Life* (Philadelphia, PA: Running Press, 2009).

Trump, Donald, *Time to Get Tough: Making America #1 Again* (Washington DC: Regnery Publishing, 2011).

Trump, Donald, *Crippled America: How to Make America Great Again* (New York: Threshold Editions, 2015).

Articles

Butterfield, Fox, "New Hampshire speech earns praise for Trump," *New York Times*, 23 October 1987.

Dowd, Maureen, "Liberties; Trump l'oeil tease," *New York Times*, 19 September 1999.

Hochman, David, "Donald Trump (good & bad)," *Playboy*, October 2004.

Plaskin, Glenn, "Donald Trump," *Playboy*, March 1990.

Romano, Lois, "Donald Trump, holding all the cards: The tower! The team! The money! The future!" *Washington Post*, 15 November 1984.

Time, "Donald Trump's speech to Aipac [Transcript]," *Time.com*, 21 March 2016.

Toynbee, Polly, "Towering Trump – The tycoon is big on himself and it has paid handsomely, but what can he do for the people?" *Guardian*, 26 May 1988.

Trump advertisement in the *Washington Post*, *New York Times* and *Boston Globe*, 2 September 1987.

Trump, Donald, "Donald Trump on the embargo and casinos," *Miami Herald*, 25 June 1999.

Trump, Donald, "Donald Trump: How I'd run the country (better)," *Esquire*, August 2004.

Wood, Gaby, "Donald Trump: The interview," *Observer*, 7 January 2007.

TV Interviews and Appearances (in chronological order)

Interview with Rona Barrett, "Rona Barrett looks at today's super rich", NBC, 6 October 1980.

Interview with Larry King, CNN, 2 September 1987.

Phil Donahue Show, WNBC, 16 December 1987.

Oprah Winfrey Show, ABC, 25 April 1988.

Interview with Shuichiro Ueyama, Japanese Television, 13 June 1988.

Late Night with David Letterman, NBC, 10 November 1988.

Interview with Robert Lipsyte, "The 11th Hour," WNET, September 1989.

Interview with Larry King, CNN, 18 April 1990.

Interview with Larry King, CNN, 8 October 1999.

Interview with Alan Marcus, WWOR-TV, 11 September 2001.

The Howard Stern Show (WXRK), 11 September 2002.

Your World With Neil Cavuto, Fox News, 28 January 2003.

Your World With Neil Cavuto, Fox News, 21 March 2003.

Scarborough Country, MSNBC, 11 September 2003.

Interview with Wolf Blitzer, CNN's "Late Edition," 21 March 2004.

Interview with Larry King, CNN, 15 April 2009.

Late Show with David Letterman, CBS, 11 March 2010.

Joy Behar Show, CNN, 8 December 2010.

Piers Morgan Tonight, CNN, 28 March 2011.

The O'Reilly Factor, Fox News, 30 March 2011.

The O'Reilly Factor, Fox News, 31 March 2011.

The O'Reilly Factor, Fox News, 1 April 2011.

State of the Union with Candy Crowley, 17 April 2011.

Interview with George Stephanopoulos, ABC News, 18 April 2011.

Interview with Xinhua (Official Chinese News Agency), 3 May 2011.

The O'Reilly Factor, Fox News, 12 December 2011.

Piers Morgan Tonight, CNN, 4 January 2012.

Piers Morgan Live, CNN, 13 June 2013.
Piers Morgan Live, CNN, 13 September 2013.
Piers Morgan Live, CNN, 10 October 2013.
Interview with Thomas Roberts, MSNBC, 9 November 2013.
Piers Morgan Live, CNN, 11 December 2013.

Speeches

Trump, Donald, Speech at Conservative Political Action Committee (CPAC) conference, 10 February 2011.
Trump, Donald, Speech to Republican women's groups in Las Vegas, Nevada, 29 April 2011.
Trump, Donald, Speech at the 2014 Conservative Political Action Conference (CSPAN), 6 March 2014.
Trump, Donald, Presidential Campaign Announcement Speech, 16 June 2015.
Trump, Donald, Republican Nomination Acceptance Speech, 21 July 2016.

Video

"From the desk of Donald Trump," video posted by The Trump Organization, uploaded on 28 February 2011. Available at https://www.facebook.com/DonaldTrump/posts/149598435099986.

NEWSPAPERS, MAGAZINES AND WEBSITES

ABC News   *Boston Globe*
The Atlantic   *Breitbart*
BBC Magazine   *CBS*

Chicago Tribune	*New York Times*
CNN	*Observer (UK)*
Financial Times	*Playboy*
Fox News	*Politico*
Guardian	*Reuters*
Jerusalem Post	*Spectator*
Los Angeles Times	*Time*
Miami Herald	*The Times (London)*
MSNBC News	*Wall Street Journal*
NBC	*Washington Post*
Newsweek	*WNBC*

SECONDARY LITERATURE

Books

Blair, Gwenda, *The Trumps: Three Generations that Built an Empire* (New York: Simon & Schuster, 2000).

Bolton, John, *Surrender is Not an Option: Defending America at the United Nations and Abroad* (New York: Threshold Editions, 2008).

Buchanan, Patrick, *A Republic Not an Empire: Reclaiming America's Destiny* (Washington DC: Regnery Publishing, 1999).

Chollet, Derek, and James Goldgeier, *America Between the Wars: From 11/9 to 9/11: The Misunderstood Years Between the Fall of the Berlin Wall and Start of the War on Terror* (New York: PublicAffairs, 2008).

D'Antonio, Michael, *Never Enough: Donald Trump and the Pursuit of Success* (New York: Thomas Dunne Books, 2015).

Doenecke, Justus D., (ed.), *In Danger Undaunted: The Anti-Interventionist Movement of 1940–1941 as Revealed in the*

Papers of the America First Committee (Stanford, CA: Hoover Institution Press, 1990).

Doenecke, Justus D., *The Battle Against Intervention, 1939–1941* (Malabar, FL, 1997).

Freedman, Lawrence, *A Choice of Enemies: America Confronts the Middle East* (London: Weidenfeld & Nicholson, 2008).

Harding, Warren G., (edited by Fredrick E. Schortemeier) *Rededicating America: Life and Recent Speeches of Warren G. Harding* (Indianapolis, 1920).

Johnston, David Cay, *The Making of Donald Trump* (Brooklyn: Melville House, 2016).

Judis, John B., *The Populist Explosion: How the Great Recession Transformed American and European Politics* (New York: Columbia Global Reports, 2016).

Kennedy, Paul, *The Rise and Fall of the Great Powers: Economic Change and Military Conflict from 1500 to 2000* (New York: Random House, 1987).

Kissinger, Henry, *White House Years* (Boston: Little Brown & Co, 1979).

Kranish, Michael, *Trump Revealed: An American Journey of Ambition, Ego, Money and Power* (New York: Scribner's 2016).

Lawrence, Mark Atwood, *The Vietnam War: A Concise International History* (New York: Oxford University Press, 2008).

Leffler, Melvyn P., *The Elusive Quest: America's Pursuit of European Stability and French Security, 1919–1933* (Chapel Hill: The University of North Carolina Press, NC, 1979).

Mead, Walter Russell, *Special Providence: American Foreign Policy and How it Changed the World* (New York: Routledge, 2001).

Olsen, Edward A., *U.S.-Japan Strategic Reciprocity: A Neo-Internationalist View* (Stanford, CA: Hoover Institution Press, 1985).

Reynolds, David, *One World Divisible: A Global History Since 1945* (New York: W.W. Norton & Company, 2000).

Seidman, Steven A., *Posters, Propaganda, and Persuasion in Election Campaigns Around the World and Through History* (New York: Peter Lang Publishing, 2008).

Slater, Robert, *No Such Thing as Over-exposure: Inside the Life and Celebrity of Donald Trump* (Upper Saddle River, NJ: Prentice Hall, 2005).

Thompson, John A., *A Sense of Power: The Roots of America's Global Role* (Ithaca, NY: Cornell University Press, 2015).

Troy, Gil, *The Reagan Revolution: A Very Short Introduction* (New York: Oxford University Press, 2009).

Tuccille, Jermoe, *Trump* (New York: D.I. Fine, 1987).

Vogel, E.F., *Japan as Number One: Lessons for America* (Cambridge: Harvard University Press, 1979).

Articles

Applebaum, Anne, "This is how the West ends," *Slate*, 4 March 2016.

Bandow, Doug, "Ripped off: What Donald Trump gets right about U.S. alliances," *Foreign Affairs*, 12 September 2016.

Barnett, Michael N., "Donald Trump's foreign policy sounds familiar – but here's what's missing," *Washington Post*, 13 November 2016.

Blyth, Mark, "Global Trumpism," *Foreign Affairs*, 15 November 2016.

Brogan, Denis Wiliam, "The Illusion of American Omnipotence," *Harper's Monthly,* December 1952.

The Chronicle Review, "Trump 101," *The Chronicle of Higher Education*, 19 June 2016.

Cillizza, Chris, "Here's what was missing from Donald Trump's foreign policy speech," *Washington Post*, 27 April 2016.

Cloud, David S., "How much do allies pay for U.S. troops? A lot more than Donald Trumps says," 1 October 2016. [http://www.latimes.com/nation/la-na-trump-allies-20160930-snap-story.html].

Connolly, N.D.B., and Blain, Keisha N., "Trump Syllabus 2.0," *Publicbooks.org*, 28 June 2016.

Drezner, Daniel W., "Let's make Donald Trump's foreign policy great again," *Washington Post*, 21 July 2016.

Drezner, Daniel W., "The doom loop of Donald Trump's foreign policy musings," *Washington Post*, 2 August 2016. [https://www.washingtonpost.com/posteverything/wp/2016/07/21/lets-make-donald-trumps-foreign-policy-great-again/].

Eichenwald, Kurt, "How Donald Trump's Company Violated the United States Embargo Against Cuba," *Newsweek*, 29 September 2016.

Farrell, Theo, "Humanitarian Intervention and Peace Operations," in John Baylis, James J. Wirtz, Colin S. Gray (eds), *Strategy in the Contemporary World* (Oxford: Oxford University Press, 2002), pp. 5–48.

Fisher, Max, "What is Donald Trump's Foreign Policy?" *The New York Times*, 11 November 2016.

Friedman, Uri, "How Donald Trump Could Change the World. An Interview with Thomas Wright," *The Atlantic*, 7 November 2016.

Fukayama, Francis, "Trump and American Political Decay," *Foreign Affairs*, 9 November 2016.

Gholz, Eugene, Daryl G. Press and Harvey M. Sapolsky (1996) "Come Home, America: The Strategy of Restraint in the Face of Temptation," *International Security*, 21/4.

Harris, Jennifer M., "The Rex Files," *Foreign Affairs*, 16 December 2016.

Heer, Jeet, "Donald Trump's Foreign Policy Revolution," *The New Republic*, 25 March 2016.

Heilbrunn, Jacob, "The GOP's New Foreign-Policy Populism," *The National Interest*, 17 February 2016.

Heisbourg, Francis, "The Future of the U.S. Alliance System," *Foreign Affairs*, 12 May 2016.

Inboden, William, "Dark Days: Trump, Christianity and a Low Dishonest Decade," *War on the Rocks*, 1 August 2016.

Kalan, Dariusz, "Central Europe's Uncertain Future," *Foreign Affairs*, 21 November 2016.

Kane, Tim, "Global U.S. Troop Deployments, 1950–2003," *Center for Data Analysis Report #04–11 on NationalSecurity and Defence, Heritage Foundation*, 27 October 2004.

Kaplan, Robert, "On foreign policy, Donald Trump is no realist," *The Washington Post*, 12 November 2016.

Kirchick, James, "How Trump Got His Party to Love Russia," *Washingtonpost.com*, 6 January 2017. [https://www.washingtonpost.com/posteverything/wp/2017/01/06/how-trump-got-his-party-to-love-russia/?utm_term=.257f8c7e94b7].

Kirchick, James, "Why Donald Trump Keeps Dissing America's Allies in Europe and Asia," *The Daily Beast*, 29 December 2016.

Klieman, Aharon and Yoel Guzansky, "Reading Trump's Middle East Policy," *Foreign Affairs*, 17 November 2016.

Kruse, Michael, "He Brutalized for You," *Politico*, 8 April 2016.

Langley, Monica, and Gerard Baker, "Donald Trump, in Exclusive Interview, Tells WSJ He is Willing to Keep Parts of Obama's Health Law," *Wall Street Journal*, 11 November 2016. Lewis, Jeffrey, "Donald Trump is an Idiot Savant On Nuclear Policy," *Foreign Policy*, 7 March 2016.

Luce, Edward, "Lunch with the FT: Roger Stone" *FT.Com*, 26 August 2016. [https://www.ft.com/content/44685c74-6ad5-11e6-a0b1-d87a9fea034f].

Mahler, Jonathan, and Matt Flegenheimer, "What Donald Trump Learned from Joseph McCarthy's Right-Hand Man," *New York Times*, 20 June 2016.

Miller, Chris, "U.S.-Russian Relations in the Next Presidency," *German Marshall Fund*, Policy Brief, 7 December 2016.

Miller, Jennifer, "Adam Smith's Arthiritis: Japan and the Fear of American Decline," Paper delivered at conference, *Ronald Reagan and the Transformation of Global Politics in the 1980s*, Austin, Texas, 20 January 2017 (paper in possession of author).

Miller, Paul D., "What Both the Left and Right Should Learn from Trump's Election," *The Federalist*, 11 November 2016.

Nolt, James H., "Is China a Currency Manipulator?," *World Policy Blog*, 14 January 2016.

Nye, Joseph, "Will the Liberal Order Survive?," *Foreign Affairs*, January/February 2017.

Rachman, Gideon, "Donald Trump, Viktor Orbán and the west's great walls," *Financial Times*, 29 February 2016.

Rose, Gideon, "Out of Order?" *Foreign Affairs*, January/February 2017.

Ryan, Missy, "Meet the men shaping Donald Trump's foreign policy views," *Chicago Tribune*, 21 March 2016.

Sanger, David E., "Envisioning Donald Trump's Foreign Policy: The U.S. Steps Back," *New York Times*, 21 July 2016.

Saunders, Elizabeth, "What a President Trump means for foreign policy," *Washington Post*, 9 November 2016.

Sestanovich, Stephen, "The Truth About Populism and Foreign Policy," *Foreign Affairs*, 30 May 2016.

Shiflett, Dave, "Another Time, Another Trump," *Wall Street Journal*, 16 December 2015.

Shifrinson, Joshua, "Donald Trump's foreign policy views are actually pretty mainstream," *Washington Post*, 4 February 2016.

Simms, Brendan, "America alone. The United States would survive a Trump presidency – but what about the rest of the world?," *New Statesman*, 7–13 October 2016, pp. 25–31.

Simms, Brendan, "A world unbalanced," *New Statesman*, 2–8 December 2016, pp. 31–4.

Stacey, Jeffrey A., "The Trump Doctrine: The View from Russia and Syria," *Foreign Affairs*, 14 November 2016.

Stromberg, Stephen, "Donald Trump's foreign policy: From incoherence to more incoherence," *The Washington Post*, 15 August 2016.

Thompson, John A., "The Appeal of 'America First' in Donald Trump's America," *E-International Relations*, 15 January 2017.

Vaisse, Justin, "Trump's International System: A Speculative Interpretation," *War on the Rocks*, 29 December 2016.

Vogel, Ezra, "Pax Nipponica?" *Foreign Affairs*, 64/4 (Spring 1986).

Ward, Alex, "America Alone: Trump's Unilateralist Foreign Policy," *War on the Rocks*, 31 May 2016.

"Washington Post Interview with Rona Barrett by Robert Samuels" in "Trump Revealed": The reporting archive, 30 August 2016.

Wertheim, Stephen, "Trump and American Exceptionalism: Why a Crippled America is Something New," *Foreign Affairs*, 3 January 2017.

White, T.H., "The Danger from Japan," *New York Times Magazine*, 28 July 1985.

Wright, Thomas, "Trump's 19th Century Foreign Policy," *Politico*, 20 January 2016.

Wright, Thomas, "Donald Trump wants America to withdraw from the world," *Financial Times*, 23 March 2016.

Wright, Thomas, "Trump's Team of Rivals, Riven by Distrust," *Foreign Policy*, 14 December 2016.

Zakaria, Fareed, "Excerpt: Zakaria's 'The Post-American World,'" *Newsweek*, 3 May 2008.

Zakaria, Fareed, "Populism on the March," *Foreign Affairs*, November/December 2016 Issue.

Zakaria, Fareed, "America's democracy has become illiberal," *The Washington Post*, 29 December 2016.

Zito, Salena, "Taking Trump Seriously, Not Literally," *The Atlantic*, 23 September 2016.

INDEX